A Barclay
Prayer Book

William Barclay

SCM PRESS LTD
London

TRINITY PRESS INTERNATIONAL
Philadelphia

This edition first published 1990.
The contents were first published by SCM Press as
Prayers for the Christian Year (1964) and
Epilogues and Prayers (1963).
Third impression 1991

SCM Press Ltd   Trinity Press International
26–30 Tottenham Road   3725 Chestnut Street
London N1 4BZ   Philadelphia Pa. 19104

British Library Cataloguing in Publication Data

Barclay, William *1907–1978*
A Barclay prayer book.
1. Anglicans. Christian life. Prayers – Devotional works
I. Title II. Barclay, William *1907–1978*. Epilogues and
prayers III. Barclay, William *1907–1978*. Prayers for the
Christian year
242.803

ISBN 0–334–02460–9

Library of Congress Cataloguing in Publication Data

Barclay, William, 1907–1978.
A Barclay prayer book / William Barclay.
p   cm
ISBN 0–334–02460–9
1. Devotional calendars. 2. Church year. I. Title.
BV4812.B3 1990
242′.3——dc20
90–39209
CIP

Printed in England by Clays Ltd, St Ives plc

CONTENTS

PREFACE

There was a profound simplicity about the best that William Barclay wrote, and that best included his *Daily Study Bible* and his prayers. Some prayers he wrote for private use, some for use in public, particularly with young people, but so personal was the stamp he put on them, that it is usually difficult to tell which are which.

This *Barclay Prayer Book* contains prayers which originally appeared in *Prayers for the Christian Year* and *Epilogues and Prayers*, both no longer available. They were written almost thirty years ago, but are still as fresh as ever – with one slight exception. Particularly since 1978, when William Barclay died, we have become aware in a way that we were not aware in the past of the way in which the language of prayer can be sexist: the most blatant example of this which appeared in *Prayers for the Christian Year* was the phrase 'Give us ministers who are men . . .', which William Barclay would certainly not have wanted to exclude women.

So for this new edition we have lightly revised all those passages which now seem too masculine: it was not a difficult task, for William Barclay's thought was always open and his sympathies wide.

Within this volume are the Collects from the Anglican Book of Common Prayer, some of the treasures of the English language. Within it, too, are modern words of the utmost directness, clarity and simplicity which nevertheless avoid that banality which is such a danger in prayer. We come to see the wellspring of spirituality which nourished William Barclay's great creativity; and we come to see what we, too, share with him. 'Prayer,' he commented, 'should be such that now and again someone will say, "This means me".' Those who use this book will have that feeling time and time again.

The order of the prayers in the first two sections follows the church's calendar as found in the Book of Common Prayer. The prayers on various themes which form the third section were originally written for an evening act of worship, but can easily be adapted for any occasion.

John Bowden, *SCM Press*

I

The Christian Year

The First Sunday in Advent

Almighty God, give us grace that we may cast away the works of darkness, and put upon us the armour of light, now in the time of this mortal life, in which thy Son Jesus Christ came to visit us in great humility; that in the last day, when he shall come again in his glorious Majesty to judge both the quick and the dead, we may rise to the life immortal, through him who liveth and reigneth with thee and the Holy Ghost, now and ever. Amen.

Epistle: Romans 13.8-14   *Gospel:* Matthew 21.1-13

O God, our Father, we thank you that you sent your Son Jesus Christ into this world to be our Saviour and our Lord.

We thank you that he took our body and our flesh and blood upon himself, and so showed us that this body of ours is fit to be your dwelling-place.

We thank you that he did our work, that he earned a living, that he served the public, and so showed us that even the smallest tasks are not beneath your majesty and can be done for you.

We thank you that he lived in an ordinary home, that he knew the problems of living together, that he experienced the rough and smooth of family life, and so showed us that any home, however humble, can be a place where in the ordinary routine of daily life we can make all life an act of worship to you.

Lord Jesus, come again to us this day.

> Come into our hearts, and so cleanse them, that we being pure in heart may see God, our Father.

> Come into our minds, and so enlighten and illumine them that we may know you who are the way, the truth, and the life.

> Touch our lips, that we may speak no word which would hurt another or grieve you.

> Touch our eyes, that they may never linger on any forbidden thing.

> Touch our hands, that they may become lovely with service to the needs of others.

> Come when we are sad, to comfort us; when we are tired, to refresh us; when we are lonely, to cheer us; when we are tempted, to strengthen us; when we are perplexed, to guide us; when we are happy, to make our joy doubly dear.

O God, our Father, help us so to live that, whenever your call comes for us, at morning, at midday or at evening, it may find us ready, our work completed, and our hearts at peace with you, so that we may enter at last with joy into your nearer presence and into life eternal; through Jesus Christ our Lord. Amen

The Second Sunday in Advent

Blessed Lord, who hast caused all holy Scriptures to be written for our learning: Grant that we may in such wise hear them, read, mark, learn, and inwardly digest them, that by patience, and comfort of thy holy Word, we may embrace, and ever hold fast the blessed hope of everlasting life, which thou hast given us in our Saviour Jesus Christ. **Amen.**

Epistle: Romans 15.4-13   *Gospel:* Luke 21.25-33

O God, this day we thank you for your Book.

> For those who wrote it, for those who lived close to you, so that you could speak to them and so give them a message for their day and for ours;
>> We thank you, O God.

> For those who translated it into our own languages, often at the cost of blood and sweat and agony and death, so that your word can speak to us in the tongue we know;
>> We thank you, O God.

> For scholars whose devoted and consecrated study and toil has opened the meaning of your Book to others;
>> We thank you, O God.

> For those who print it and publish it, and for the great Bible Societies whose work makes it possible for the poorest of people all over the world to possess your word;
>> We thank you, O God.

10

For its thrilling stories of high and gallant adventure;
For its poetry which lingers for ever in the memory of
men and women;
For its teaching about how to live and how to act and
how to speak;
For its record of human thoughts about you and about
our blessed Lord;
For its comfort in sorrow, for its guidance in per-
plexity, for its hope in despair;
Above all else for its picture of Jesus:
We thank you, O God.
Make us at all times
Constant in reading it;
Glad to listen to it;
Eager to study it;
Retentive to remember it;
Resolute to obey it.

And so grant that in searching the Scriptures we may find
life for ourselves and for others; through Jesus Christ our
Lord. Amen.

The Third Sunday in Advent

O Lord Jesus Christ, who at thy first coming didst send thy messenger to prepare thy way before thee: Grant that the ministers and stewards of thy mysteries may likewise so prepare and make ready thy way, by turning the hearts of the disobedient to the wisdom of the just, that at thy second coming to judge the world we may be found an acceptable people in thy sight, who livest and reignest with the Father and the Holy Spirit, ever one God, world without end. Amen.

Epistle: I Corinthians 4.1-5   *Gospel:* Matthew 11.2-10

Lord Jesus, in your days in the body in Palestine you chose followers that you might send them out to do your work. We know that you are still looking for hands and voices and minds to use, and we ask you to bless those whom you are still sending out on your service.

> Bless the ministers of your Church in all its branches. Make them diligent in study, faithful in pastoral duty, wise in teaching, fearless and winsome in preaching, and ever clothed with your grace and love.

> Bless those who teach the young in schools, and colleges, and universities. Make them to think adventurously and to teach enthusiastically, that they may kindle and inspire young minds in the search for truth. Help them to be such that they may infect others with the contagion of the love of learning, dedicated to the service of the world.

Bless those who heal and tend the sick, doctors, surgeons and nurses. Give them skill, gentleness and sympathy, so that, when it is possible to heal, they may do so, and, when it is not possible, they may bring help and comfort to those who enter into the valley of the shadow.

Bless fathers and mothers to whom you have committed the trust of a little child. Help them to build a home in which wise discipline and understanding walk hand in hand.

Bless those who do the world's work, and grant that whatever they do they may do for you, so that they may never offer less than their best, and so that they may have no need to be ashamed.

So grant that all your servants, faithfully serving you and their fellow men and women, may prepare themselves and those amongst whom they work for your coming again.
This we ask for your love's sake. Amen.

The Fourth Sunday in Advent

O Lord, raise up (we pray thee) thy power, and come among us, and with great might succour us; that whereas, through our sins and wickedness, we are sore let and hindered in running the race that is set before us, thy bountiful grace and mercy may speedily help and deliver us; through the satisfaction of thy Son our Lord, to whom with thee and the Holy Ghost be honour and glory, world without end. Amen.

Epistle: Philippians 4.4-7   *Gospel:* John 1.19-28

Lord Jesus, send to us the power, the might, the grace, which we need so much to help us to overcome sin and to conquer our temptations.

> The purity of heart which will shut the door of our minds to every evil thought;
> The strength of will which will make us able to defy all temptations;
> The human love which will banish for ever all bitterness, and which will make us to serve as you served, and to forgive as you forgave:
> > Grant us these things.

> The fidelity on which others can utterly rely;
> The diligence which will never offer less than its best;
> The will to work which hates all lazy idleness:
> > Grant us these things.

> The power of decision which will deliver us from all procrastination;

14

The perseverance which will refuse to leave anything half done;
The courage to face the tasks we fear and do not want to do:
Grant us these things.

Grant that we may neither be too much lost in regrets for the past or dreams for the future, but grant that we may do with our might that which lies to our hand, so that we may fight the good fight, and finish the race, and keep the faith, and so at the end receive the crown of righteousness which you will award to those who have been faithful.

This we ask for your love's sake. Amen.

Christmas Day and the Sunday after Christmas Day

Almighty God, who hast given us thy only-begotten Son to take our nature upon him, and as at this time to be born of a pure Virgin: Grant that we being regenerate, and made thy children by adoption and grace, may daily be renewed by thy Holy Spirit; through the same our Lord Jesus Christ, who liveth and reigneth with thee and the same Spirit, ever one God, world without end. Amen.

Christmas-Day:

Epistle: Hebrews 1.1-12   *Gospel:* John 1.1-14

The Sunday after Christmas-Day:

Epistle: Galatians 4.1-7   *Gospel:* Matthew 1.18-25

O God, our Father, we remember at this Christmas time how the eternal Word became flesh and dwelt among us.

We thank you that Jesus took our human body upon him, so that we can never again dare to despise or neglect or misuse the body, since you made it your dwelling-place.

We thank you that Jesus did a day's work like any working-man, that he knew the problem of living together in a family, that he knew the frustration and irritation of serving the public, that he had to earn a living, and to face all the wearing routine of everyday work and life and living, and so clothed each common task with glory.

16

We thank you that he shared in all happy social occasions, that he was at home at weddings and at dinners and at festivals in the homes of simple ordinary people like ourselves. Grant that we may ever remember that in his unseen risen presence he is a guest in every home.

We thank you that he knew what friendship means, that he had his own circle of those whom he wanted to be with him, that he knew too what it means to be let down, to suffer from disloyalty and from the failure of love.

We thank you that he too had to bear unfair criticism, prejudiced opposition, malicious and deliberate misunderstanding.

We thank you that whatever happens to us, he has been there before, and that, because he himself has gone through things, he is able to help those who are going through them.

Help us never to forget that he knows life, because he lived life, and that he is with us at all times to enable us to live victoriously.

This we ask for your love's sake. Amen.

Saint Stephen's Day

*Grant, O Lord, that in all our sufferings here upon earth
for the testimony of thy truth, we may stedfastly look up to
heaven, and by faith behold the glory that shall be revealed;
and, being filled with the Holy Ghost, may learn to love and
bless our persecutors by the example of thy first Martyr
Saint Stephen, who prayed for his murderers to thee, O
blessed Jesus, who standest at the right hand of God to
succour all those that suffer for thee, our only Mediator and
Advocate.* Amen.

Lesson: Acts 7.55-60   *Gospel:* Matthew 23.34-49

O God, our Father, help us ever to see eternity beyond time.
When loyalty to Jesus brings suffering and trial,

> Help us to remember,
>> That we walk in the footsteps of the saints and the
>> martyrs;
>> That our reward in heaven is great, for you will
>> be in no one's debt;
>> That beyond the cross there waits the crown;
>> That through it all we have the promise that he
>> is with us always to the end of the world and
>> beyond.

Give us grace, O God, to love and to pray even for those
who hurt and wrong us.

Grant, O God of love,

> That injury may not awaken in us the desire for revenge;
>
> That injustice may not embitter us;
>
> That unfair criticism and even slander may not enrage us.

But grant that,

> We may meet hatred with love,
>
> And injury with forgiveness.

To that end make us at all times to look to our Blessed Lord at your right hand and to remember,

> that there is nothing which we must suffer
> that he has not already suffered;
> that because he has gone through it,
> he can help others who are going through it.

Lord Jesus, help us to bear your cross that we may share your crown. This we ask for your love's sake. Amen

Saint Stephen's Day is 26th December.

Saint John the Evangelist's Day

Merciful Lord, we beseech thee to cast thy bright beams of light upon thy Church, that it being enlightened by the doctrine of thy blessed Apostle and Evangelist Saint John may so walk in the light of thy truth, that it may at length attain to the light of everlasting life; through Jesus Christ our Lord. Amen.

Epistle: 1 John 1.1-10   *Gospel:* John 21.19-25

O God, our Father, give light to your whole Church and give light to each one of us.

Give us light that we may believe aright.
> So grant
>> That our beliefs may be right, certain, and true;
>> That no heresy and no false doctrine may disturb or destroy the faith;
>> That no self-will may blind us to the truth, making us wilfully refuse to see the things we ought to see.

Give us light that we may walk aright.
> So grant
>> That the light of truth may show us where we ought to go;
>> That the knowledge of the truth may guide us in all our decisions;
>> That we may ever walk with him who is the Way, the Truth, and the Life.

Grant that we may seek the truth aright.
So grant
> That we may seek the truth in the Gospel and the Letters of your Apostle John and in the whole Bible;
>
> That we may never be deaf to the voice of conscience or to the promptings of the Holy Spirit;
>
> That we may turn to you for guidance so that we may be guided where we cannot see.

Grant that we may reach the light of everlasting life.
So grant
> That guided by your light we may reach the light that never fades;
>
> That illumined by your truth we may reach the truth which is complete;
>
> That in the end we may see light in your light and know even as also we are known.

This we ask through Jesus Christ our Lord. Amen.

Saint John the Evangelist's Day is 27th December.

The Innocents' Day

O Almighty God, who out of the mouths of babes and sucklings hast ordained strength, and madest infants to glorify thee by their deaths: Mortify and kill all vices in us, and so strengthen us by thy grace, that by the innocency of our lives, and constancy of our faith even unto death, we may glorify thy holy Name; through Jesus Christ our Lord. Amen.

Lesson: Revelation 14.1-5   *Gospel:* Matthew 2.13-18

O God, our Father, this day we remember the little children who suffered by the cruelty of men in the days when Jesus, our blessed Lord, was born a child into this world.

This day we ask you to give us a childlike heart.

Give us,

> A child's innocence,
>> that we may be numbered with the pure in heart;
>
> A child's wonder,
>> that the loveliness of the world
>>> may be to us for ever new;
>
> A child's forgiveness,
>> that we may forget injustice and unfairness,
>>> as a child forgets;
>
> A child's obedience,
>> that as a child obeys a father,
>>> we may obey you;
>
> A child's trust,
>> that as a child trusts his parents for everything,
>> we may commit our lives in trust to you.

This day we ask you to give us a faithful heart.

Give us a heart
    So loyal,
        that we will never be ashamed to show,
            whose we are and whom we serve;
    So true to you,
        that we will remain true,
            even if we have to stand alone;
    So faithful to you,
        that no temptation and no seduction
            may ever lure us from your path.

And, if our fidelity should cost us something, make us glad for the opportunity to show how much we love you; through Jesus Christ our Lord. Amen.

The Innocents' Day is 28th December.

The Circumcision of Christ

Almighty God, who madest thy blessed Son to be circumcised, and obedient to the law for man: Grant us the true Circumcision of the Spirit; that, our hearts, and all our members, being mortified from all worldly and carnal lusts, we may in all things obey thy blessed will; through the same thy Son Jesus Christ our Lord. Amen.

Epistle: Romans 4.8-14   *Gospel:* Luke 2.15-21

O God, our Father, help us to express our religion, not in outward rituals and ceremonies and conventions, but in the inner devotion of our hearts, and in the true and ungrudging service of you and of our fellow men and women.

Make us to remember that no pious obedience to conventional acts can ever be a substitute for the love which expresses itself in sympathy and in practical help.

Make us to realize that consistent attendance at the services of your Church, diligent study of your Book and your word, even discipline in prayer itself, must all go for nothing, unless they make our daily life at work, on the streets, in the home, more like the life of Jesus in his love.

Save us from being religious in church, and at the same time cross, ill-tempered, moody, difficult to live with at home.

Save us from being meticulous in Bible study and in prayer, and at the same time slack, careless and inefficient at our work.

24

Save us from going through all the motions of religion on Sunday, and at the same time being self-centred, bitter, unforgiving, intolerant, proud, careless of the feelings and the needs of others on Monday.

So cleanse and purify us that, not only our outward actions, but even the inmost thoughts of our hearts may be pure. So remake us that we may not only not do any wrong thing, but that we not even want to do it.

All this we ask through Jesus Christ our Lord. Amen.

The Circumcision is commemorated on 1st January.

The Epiphany, or the Manifestation of Christ to the Gentiles

O God, who by the leading of a star didst manifest thy only-begotten Son to the Gentiles: Mercifully grant, that we, which know thee now by faith, may after this life have the fruition of thy glorious Godhead; through Jesus Christ our Lord. Amen.

Epistle: Ephesians 3.1-12   *Gospel:* Matthew 2.1-12

O God, our Father, who in the ancient days led men from the ends of the earth to the manger-cradle of Jesus, your Son, our Lord, we know that you want everyone to be saved. We know that Jesus said that, if he was lifted up from the earth, he would draw everyone to him. Grant that the time may soon come when those of every race and nation will know you and love you and serve you.

> We thank you that we have been brought up in a land in which the Bible is open to us and in which the Church welcomes us, in which we possess liberty of conscience and freedom of speech and worship.

> Help us always to remember those who do not possess the blessings which we enjoy:
>> Those who have never heard the name of Jesus;
>> Those who have had the glimpses of the light which everyone has, but who have never seen him who is the true light of the world;
>> Those who live in lands where there is no freedom, and where they are persecuted for their faith.

Bless those who have gone out to take Christ to all
such places.

In their loneliness, cheer them;

In their dangers, protect them;

In their discouragements, give them unconquer-
able hope;

And, if they have had to leave behind them wife
and child and family in order to go out into the
distant places, give them joy in your own presence and company.

Help us who remain at home to be ungrudging in
giving and unwearied in service that those who
have gone out may be supported in their God-given
task of spreading your gospel.

So bring nearer the day when everyone will know you and
love you; when the knowledge of you will cover the earth
as the waters cover the sea; when the kingdoms of the world
will be your kingdom and the kingdom of your Christ.

This we ask through Jesus Christ our Lord. Amen.

The First Sunday after the Epiphany

O Lord, we beseech thee mercifully to receive the prayers of thy people which call upon thee; and grant that they may both perceive and know what things they ought to do, and also may have grace and power faithfully to fulfil the same; through Jesus Christ our Lord. Amen.

Epistle: Romans 12.1-5   *Gospel:* Luke 2.41-52

O God, our Father, give us wisdom to know what we ought to do.

Save us from
>   The cowardice which will not face the truth;
>   The laziness which will not learn the truth;
>   The prejudice which cannot see the truth;
>   The stubbornness which will not accept the truth;
>   The pride which will not seek the truth.

Save us from
>   The folly that is deaf to conscience;
>   The arrogance which will not accept advice;
>   The self-conceit which resents all rebuke;
>   The shut mind that bars the door to the entry of the Holy Spirit, who is the Spirit of truth.

O God, our Father, give us grace and power to do what we ought to do.

Save us from
>   The weakness of will which is too easily deflected from its goal;

The lack of resistance which too easily yields to temptation;

The procrastination which puts things off until it is too late to do them;

The want of perseverance which begins a task but cannot finish it.

Save us from

The love of ease which chooses the comfortable way;

The fear of others which cannot stand alone;

The faint heart which will not venture for your name.

So grant us wisdom clearly to know and power faithfully to fulfil your commands; through Jesus Christ our Lord. Amen.

The Second Sunday after the Epiphany

Almighty and everlasting God, who dost govern all things in heaven and earth: Mercifully hear the supplications of thy people, and grant us thy peace all the days of our life; through Jesus Christ our Lord. Amen.

Epistle: Romans 12.6-16   *Gospel:* John 2.1-11

Father of peace and God of love, grant us your peace.

Send your peace to the world.

Take from the world the threat of war, and bring in the time when the nations will live in friendship with each other, united as subjects of that Kingdom of which you are King, and as members of that Family of which you are Father. Give us strength and grace, faith and courage to build a world in which there are no national barriers, no political divisions, no iron curtains, no dividing walls, no colour bar, but in which all are one in Jesus Christ.

Send your peace to our country.

Help those in politics to set the state above the party, and to set your will above all else.

In industry take away all suspicion and distrust. Remind workers of the pride of craftsmanship and the desire to become those who have never any need to be ashamed of their work. Make employers to see their responsibilities to their employees, and make employees to see their duty to their employers, that all may work in brotherhood together for the common good.

Send peace within ourselves.

Help us to live in peace with our fellow men and women.

Rid us of the bitter and the unforgiving spirit. Control our temper and our tongue. Grant that we may nourish no grudge within our hearts and no memory of injury within our minds, and grant that brotherly and sisterly love may banish hate.

Give us within our own hearts the peace that passes understanding.

Take from us the worries which distract us, and give us more trust.

Take from us the doubts which disturb us, and make us more sure of what we believe.

Take from us the wrong desires from which our temptations come, and make us more pure in heart.

Take from us the false ambitions which drive us, and make us more content to serve you where we are and as we are.

Take from us all estrangement from you and give us the peace of sins forgiven.

All this we ask through Jesus Christ our Lord. Amen.

The Third Sunday after the Epiphany

Almighty and everlasting God, mercifully look upon our infirmities, and in all our dangers and necessities stretch forth thy right hand to help and defend us; through Jesus Christ our Lord. Amen.

Epistle: Romans 12.16-21   *Gospel:* Matthew 8.1-13

O God, our Father, we know so well the infirmity and the weakness of this human life.

> Strengthen the weakness of our faith, and give us trust for our trembling and hope for our fears.
>
> Strengthen the weakness of our wills, that we may ever be strong enough to choose the right and to resist the wrong.
>
> Strengthen the weakness of our decision, that we may no longer halt between two opinions.
>
> Strengthen the weakness of our loyalty, that we may never again be ashamed to show whose we are and whom we serve.
>
> Strengthen the weakness of our love, that we may come at last to love you as you have first loved us.

O God, our Father, we know so well the weakness of our bodies.

> Keep us in good health; but, if illness and pain come to us, give us patience and cheerful endurance and healing in the end. And, as the years take from us strength of body, give us peace of heart and serenity of mind.

O God, our Father, we know so well the weakness and the insecurity of our hold upon this life.

> In life we are in the midst of death. Comfort us when dear and loved ones are taken from us, and at such a time give us the glorious and immortal hope of life eternal as well as the sad memories of mortal loss. And deliver us from the fear of death, so that we may look on death as the gateway to eternal life for ever with our Lord.

Grant us all through life your all-sufficient grace that your power may ever be made perfect in our weakness; through Jesus Christ our Lord. Amen.

The Fourth Sunday after the Epiphany

O God, who knowest us to be set in the midst of so many and great dangers, that by reason of the frailty of our nature we cannot always stand upright: Grant to us such strength and protection, as may support us in all dangers, and carry us through all temptations; through Jesus Christ our Lord. Amen.

Epistle: Romans 13.1-7   *Gospel:* Matthew 8.23-34

O God, our Father, help us to resist the temptations which continually attack us.

Help us to resist the temptations which come from within and from our own natures:

> The temptation to laziness and to too much love of ease and comfort;
> The temptation to pride and self-conceit and to think of ourselves more highly than we ought;
> The temptation to put things off until it is too late ever to do them, and to refuse to face the unpleasant things, until it is too late to do anything about them:
>> Help us to resist these, O God.

> The temptation to despair, and to lose heart and hope;
> The temptation to lower our standards and to accept things as they are;
> The temptation to be resignedly content with life as it is and ourselves as we are:
>> Help us to resist these, O God.

34

The temptation to let passion and desire have their way;

The temptation to trade eternal happiness for the fleeting thrill of some seductive moment;

The temptation to moodiness, to irritability, to bad temper;

The temptation to criticism, to fault-finding, to thinking the worst of others:

Help us to resist these, O God.

Help us to resist the temptations which come to us from outside.

Help us to say No to every voice which invites us to leave your way.

Help us to resist every seduction which makes sin more attractive.

Help us to walk through the world, and yet to keep our garments unspotted from the world.

Help us to be wise enough never to play with fire; never to flirt with temptation; never recklessly to put ourselves into a situation in which it is easy to go wrong; never unthinkingly to develop habits which provide an opportunity for sin.

Grant unto us that grace which will give us the strength and the purity ever to overcome evil and to do the right; through Jesus Christ our Lord. Amen.

The Fifth Sunday after the Epiphany

O Lord, we beseech thee to keep thy Church and household continually in thy true religion; that they who do lean only upon the hope of thy heavenly grace may evermore be defended by thy mighty power; through Jesus Christ our Lord. Amen.

Epistle: Colossians 3.12-17   *Gospel:* Matthew 13.24-30

O God, our Father, bless your Church,

> Give her such a passion for human souls, that she will never be content until all men and women shall know your love in Jesus Christ.
>
> Give her such a passion for social justice that she will ever be the conscience of the nation, and that she will engage upon a continuous crusade for everything that will benefit human bodies as well as human souls. Give her the conviction that each day is the Lord's Day, and so grant that she may be involved in every day's work and not only in one day's worship.
>
> Give her the adventurous spirit which refuses to be shackled to the past and which finds in tradition, not a deadweight, but an inspiration.
>
> Make her adventurous in thought that she may rethink and restate the eternal gospel in terms that all can understand.

> Make her adventurous in action, so that she may not
> shrink from that which is new, and so that she may
> not rest content in a comfortable inertia.
> Make her a fellowship in which all social and racial
> distinctions have ceased to exist.
> Give her that true sympathy and tolerance which recog-
> nize that there are as many ways to the stars as there
> are those to climb them.
> Give her at last that unity in which all barriers are
> broken down, in which all people can worship to-
> gether again, and in which the body of Christ will be
> truly one.

Grant that the Church may be a place where boys and girls find Jesus as their friend; where young men and maidens glimpse the vision splendid; where those in the midtime find a rod and a staff for the dust and the heat of the day; where those far down the vale of years find light at eventide; where the sorrowing find comfort and the weary rest; where the doubting find certainty and the tempted strength; where the lonely find fellowship and the sinner forgiveness for his sins.

Hear this our prayer, through Jesus Christ our Lord. Amen.

The Sixth Sunday after the Epiphany

O God, whose blessed Son was manifested that he might destroy the works of the devil, and make us the sons of God, and heirs of eternal life: Grant us, we beseech thee, that, having this hope, we may purify ourselves, even as he is pure; that, when he shall appear again with power and great glory, we may be made like unto him in his eternal and glorious kingdom; where with thee, O Father, and thee, O Holy Ghost, he liveth and reigneth, ever one God, world without end. Amen.

Epistle: I John 3.1-8   *Gospel:* Matthew 24.23-31

O God, our Father, we thank you for Jesus Christ our Lord, and for the great hope that he has given to us.

> For the victory he has won;
>> That he himself defeated the attacks of the Tempter,
>>> And that he can enable us also
>> To overcome evil and to do the right;
> For the sonship that he has given to us;
>> That he has brought us within your household and your family;
> For the life he has opened to us;
>> That in this world
>>> He has given us life and life more abundant,
>> That in the world to come
>>> He has promised us everlasting life:
>>>> We thank you, O God.

Grant to us the purity which is his.

Grant that
    He may reign within our hearts,
      So that every evil emotion and desire
        May be banished from them;
    He may direct our minds,
      So that all our thoughts may be right;
    He may govern our actions,
      So that we may do no wrong thing;
    He may control our speech,
      So that we may speak no word
        Which is evil, false or impure.

So grant that, victorious with his victory, pure with his purity, and living with his life, we may not be ashamed at his appearing.

This we ask for your love's sake. Amen.

The Sunday called Septuagesima, or the Third Sunday before Lent

O Lord, we beseech thee favourably to hear the prayers of thy people; that we, who are justly punished for our offences, may be mercifully delivered by thy goodness, for the glory of thy Name; through Jesus Christ our Saviour, who liveth and reigneth with thee and the Holy Ghost, ever one God, world without end. Amen.

Epistle: I Corinthians 9.24-27   *Gospel:* Matthew 20.1-16

O God, you are the King and the Judge of all the earth. You are altogether good and altogether pure. We are stained with sin, lost in error, sunk in failure. If you were to give us what we deserve, we could expect nothing but condemnation, nothing but punishment, nothing but banishment for ever from your sight.

We have disobeyed your commandments,
    And have taken our own way;
The voice of conscience has spoken,
    And we have disregarded it;
We have seen the example of the good and godly,
    And we have not followed it;
We have received the advice and the counsel, the warning and the rebuke of those who are wise,
    And we have spurned them;
Experience has shown us the damage that self-will can do,
    And we have not learned from it;

We have wished to rule,
    And not to serve;
We have wished to avenge ourselves,
    And not to forgive;
We have wished to get,
    And not to give;
We have been silent,
    When we should have spoken;
We have rushed into speech,
    When we should have been silent;
We have been selfish and unkind in our homes;
    We have been slack and inefficient in our work;
We have been careless and irresponsible in our
pleasure;
    We have been cold and neglectful in our devotion;
We have known what is right,
    And we have done what is wrong.

But we know that you are not only just and holy, but that
you are also kind. Forgive us, not because of our merit, for
we have none, but because of your love. Forgive us, not
because of our goodness, for we have none, but because of
your mercy. Take us just as we are, and forgive us for the
past, and recreate us for the future. We only dare to ask
this because of the love you have shown us in Jesus Christ
our Saviour and our Blessed Lord.

Hear this our prayer for your love's sake. Amen.

The Sunday called Sexagesima, or the Second Sunday before Lent

O Lord God, who seest that we put not our trust in any thing that we do: Mercifully grant that by thy power we may be defended against all adversity; through Jesus Christ our Lord. Amen.

Epistle: II Corinthians 11.19-31   *Gospel:* Luke 8.4-15

O God, our Father, we know that by ourselves we can do nothing.

> If we try to face our work by ourselves,
>> we collapse beneath our burdens and our responsibilities. Our bodies become exhausted; our minds grow weary; our nerves are tensed beneath the strain.
>
> If we try to face our temptations by ourselves,
>> the fascination of the wrong things is too strong. Our resistance is defeated, and we do the things we know that we should never do, because we cannot help it.
>
> If we try to face our sorrows by ourselves,
>> there is nothing to heal the wound upon our hearts, nothing to dry the fountain of our tears, nothing to comfort the loneliness which is more than we can bear.
>
> If we try to face our problems by ourselves,
>> we cannot see the right way; and, even when we see it, we cannot take it; and, even when we take it, we cannot follow it to the end.

If we try to rid ourselves of faults by ourselves,
we are for ever defeated; the same sins conquer
us; and we are never any farther on.

We know our need. Life has taught us that we cannot walk alone. So be with us to help, to guide, to comfort, to sustain, that in all the changes and the chances of life, whatever light may shine or shadow fall, we may meet life with steady eyes, and walk in wisdom and in strength, in purity and in joy in the way everlasting, until we reach our journey's end; through Jesus Christ our Lord. Amen.

Lord's PRAYER

The Sunday called Quinquagesima, or the Next Sunday before Lent

O Lord, who hast taught us that all our doings without charity are nothing worth: Send thy Holy Ghost and pour into our hearts that most excellent gift of charity, the very bond of peace and of all virtues, without which whosoever liveth is counted dead before thee; Grant this for thine only Son Jesus Christ's sake. Amen.

Epistle: I Corinthians 13   *Gospel:* Luke 18.31-43

Eternal and ever blessed God, whose name is love, put your own love into our hearts; and help us to love you as you have first loved us.

> Help us to love you so much, that we may fear nothing except to grieve you and that we may desire nothing except to please you.
>
> Help us to love you so much, that we may obey you, not as a slave obeys his master, not even as a soldier obeys his commander, but as a loved one obeys his lover.
>
> Help us to love you so much, that the worship of your house may be to us neither a burden or a duty, but a joy and a delight.
>
> Help us to love you so much in answer to your love for us, that we too may say:
>
> > Were the whole realm of nature mine,
> > That were an offering far too small;
> > Love so amazing, so divine,
> > Demands my life, my soul, my all.

Help us, O Lover of human souls, to love our fellow men and women as you love them.

Help us to love them so much, that we shall always be ready to help and always quick to forgive.

Help us to love them so much, that hatred and bitterness may no longer have any place within our hearts.

Help us to love them so much, that all shall know that we are your disciples, because we have love one for another.

All this we ask for your love's sake. Amen.

The First Day of Lent, commonly called Ash Wednesday

Almighty and everlasting God, who hatest nothing that thou hast made, and dost forgive the sins of all them that are penitent: Create and make in us new and contrite hearts, that we worthily lamenting our sins, and acknowledging our wretchedness, may obtain of thee, the God of all mercy, perfect remission and forgiveness; through Jesus Christ our Lord. Amen.

Lesson: Joel 2.12-17   *Gospel:* Matthew 6.16-21

O God, Creator and Father of all, we know that your love is over every creature whom your hands have made. We know that your only wish is not to destroy but to save, not to condemn but to forgive. And we know that, if we would receive your forgiveness, the only thing that we can bring, and the only thing that we need to bring, to you is the penitent and the contrite heart. Save us from everything which would hinder us from having a godly sorrow for our sins.

Save us, O God,
 From the blindness,
  which is not even aware that it is sinning;
 From the pride,
  which cannot admit that it is wrong;
 From the self-will,
  which can see nothing but its own way;
 From the self-righteousness,
  which can see no flaw within itself;

From the callousness,
  which has sinned so often that it has ceased to
  care;
From the defiance,
  which is not even sorry for its sins;
From the evasion,
  which always puts the blame on some one or on
  some thing else;
From the heart so hardened,
  that it cannot repent.
Give us at all times
  Eyes which are open to our own faults;
  A conscience which is sensitive and quick to warn;
  A heart which cannot sin in peace,
    but which is moved to regret and to remorse.
So grant that being truly penitent we may be truly forgiven,
so that we may find that your love is great enough to cover
all our sin; through Jesus Christ our Lord. Amen.

The Ash Wednesday Collect is used throughout Lent.

The First Sunday in Lent

O Lord, who for our sake didst fast forty days and forty nights: Give us grace to use such abstinence, that, our flesh being subdued to the Spirit, we may ever obey thy godly motions in righteousness, and true holiness, to thy honour and glory, who livest and reignest with the Father and the Holy Ghost, one God, world without end. Amen.

Epistle: II Corinthians 6.1-10   *Gospel:* Matthew 4.1-11

O Lord Jesus Christ, give us in all our life the discipline which will enable us to walk in your footsteps, and which all your true followers should show.

> Help us to discipline our passions and desires, that we may never in an unguarded moment do that which we would afterwards regret.
>
> Help us to discipline our appetites, that greed and gluttony and self-indulgence may have no part in our lives.
>
> Help us to discipline our speech, that no false or untrue word, no soiled or impure word, no bitter or angry word may ever pass our lips.
>
> Help us to discipline ourselves in our work, that slackness, idleness, laziness and carelessness may find no place in our lives, that we may not try to find how quickly we can do a thing but how well we can do it, that we may be more concerned with how much we can put into a task than with how much we can get out of it.

Help us to discipline ourselves in our pleasure, that no pleasure may ever so master us that it takes away the will-power to resist it.

Help us to discipline ourselves in our devotion, that we may faithfully share in the public worship of your people, and that no day may ever pass when in the silence we do not speak and listen to you.

Help us to discipline even our thoughts, that they may never move in any forbidden pathways or linger on any forbidden thing, so that we too may be pure in heart and so see you.

This we ask for your love's sake. Amen.

The Second Sunday in Lent

*Almighty God, who seest that we have no power of our-
selves to help ourselves: Keep us both outwardly in our
bodies, and inwardly in our souls; that we may be defended
from all adversities which may happen to the body, and
from all evil thoughts which may assault and hurt the soul;
through Jesus Christ our Lord.* Amen.

Epistle: I Thessalonians 4.1-8   *Gospel:* Matthew 15.21-28

O God, our Father, you have shown us in the works and
words of Jesus, your Son, that you care both for our bodies
and our souls. Protect us alike in body and in soul.

We pray for your blessing on our bodies.
> Health for our day's work;
> Wisdom to seek the doctor's skill, if we know, or
> even suspect, that anything is wrong;
> Wisdom neither to overdrive our bodies until we ex-
> haust them, nor to allow them to grow weak and
> flabby through too much ease;
> Wise discipline in our habits, that we may allow
> ourselves no indulgences nor become the victim
> of any habits which would injure our health:
> > Grant this, O God.

And since we know that mind and body are linked in-
separably together, grant us a sound mind:
> A mind at rest and at peace;
> A mind undistressed by worry, and free from
> anxiety;

50

A mind cleansed and purified from every evil, every
bitter and every resentful thought;
A mind determined to do all it can, and then content
to leave the rest to you :
Grant this, O God.

We pray for your blessing on our souls.
From being so immersed in the world that we forget
that we have a soul;
From being so busy with the things which are seen
and temporal that we entirely forget the things
which are unseen and eternal;
From forgetting that it does not profit us if we gain
the whole world if in so doing we lose our soul :
Save us, O God.

From the temptations which attack our soul from inside and from outside;
From all habits and practices and ways of life which
make our soul less sensitive to you;
From all that makes our soul less fit to enter your
presence when this life ends :
Defend us, O God.

Bless us in body, soul and spirit that we may live this life
well, and at the end of it enter into life eternal; through
Jesus Christ our Lord. Amen.

The Third Sunday in Lent

We beseech thee, Almighty God, look upon the hearty desires of thy humble servants, and stretch forth the right hand of thy Majesty, to be our defence against all our enemies; through Jesus Christ our Lord. Amen.

Epistle: Ephesians 5.1-14   *Gospel:* Luke 11.14-28

O God, you are the help of the helpless. You can cover our defenceless head with the shadow of your wing. It is for your defence and protection that we ask today.

Defend us from our temptations,
   That in your power,
      We may ever accept the right and refuse the
         wrong,
      We may ever overcome all evil and do the right.
Defend us from ourselves
   That in your power,
      Our weaknesses may not bring us to shame,
      Our lower nature may never seize the upper hand.
Defend us from all that would seduce us into sin,
   That in your power,
      No tempting voice may make us listen,
      No tempting sight may fascinate our eyes.
Defend us against the changes and the chances of this
life,
   Not that we may escape them,
      But that we may meet them with head erect and
         with steady eyes;

Not that we may be saved from then,
  But that we may come triumphantly through
  them.
Defend us alike
  From discouragement in difficulty, and from despair
  in failure;
  From pride in success and from forgetting you in the
  day of prosperity.
Help us to remember that
  There is no time,
    When you will fail us,
  And no moment,
    When we do not need you.

So grant that guided by your light and defended by your grace we may come in safety and in honour to our journey's end; through Jesus Christ our Lord. Amen.

The Fourth Sunday in Lent

Grant, we beseech thee, Almighty God, that we, who for our evil deeds do worthily deserve to be punished, by the comfort of thy grace may mercifully be relieved; through our Lord and Saviour Jesus Christ. Amen.

Epistle: Galatians 4.21-31   *Gospel:* John 6.1-14

O God, we thank you that you have not treated us as we deserve.

We thank you that, though you are Creator, Judge and King, you are also Father, so that, though we are wandering children, there is always a road back to our Father's house.

You have spoken to us,
   In the voice of conscience,
   In the words of your Book,
   In the promptings of your Holy Spirit,
      And yet we have not obeyed your voice.

You have shown us the best,
   In the ideals which still haunt us,
   In the life and example of the godly,
   In the pattern of Jesus,
      And yet we have not followed it.

You have tried to teach us,
   In the events of history,
   In the experiences of life,

54

In the wisdom of the sages, the prophets and the
saints,
   And yet we have not learned your lesson.

You have called us to the life of love,
   To the forgiving of each other,
   To the helping of those in need,
   To the caring which is like your care,
      And yet we have lived in bitterness, in selfish-
         ness and in heedlessness of the appeal of need.

We have nothing in our hands to bring. We have no merits
of our own. There is no plea of self-defence that we can
offer. So above all else we thank you for Jesus Christ our
Saviour, who died that we might be forgiven. So for his
sake hear us as we say: God be merciful to me a sinner.

         And when you hear,
         Forgive and save.

This we ask for your love's sake. Amen.

The Fifth Sunday in Lent

We beseech thee, Almighty God, mercifully to look upon thy people; that by thy great goodness they may be governed and preserved evermore, both in body and soul; through Jesus Christ our Lord. Amen.

Epistle: Hebrews 9.11-15   *Gospel:* John 8.46-59

O God, our Father, direct and control us in every part of our life.

> Control our tongues,
>> that we may speak no false, no angry, no impure word.
>
> Control our actions,
>> that we may do nothing to shame ourselves or to injure anyone else.
>
> Control our minds,
>> that we may think no evil, no bitter, no irreverent thought.
>
> Control our hearts,
>> that they may never be set on any wrong thing, and that they may ever love only the highest and the best.

O God, our Father, to whom the issues of life and death belong, preserve us from all ills.

> Preserve us in health of body,
>> that we may be able to earn a living for ourselves and for those whom we love.

Preserve us in soundness of mind,
    that all our judgments and decisions may be sane and wise.
Preserve us in purity of life,
    that we may conquer all temptation and ever do the right,
    that we may walk through the world and yet keep our garments unspotted from the world.

And if illness, misfortune, sorrow come to us, preserve us in courage, in endurance, and in serenity of faith, that, in all the changes and the chances of life, we may still face life with steady eyes, because we face life with you.

This we ask for your love's sake. Amen.

The Sunday, Monday, Tuesday, Wednesday and Thursday before Easter

Almighty and everlasting God, who, of thy tender love towards mankind, hast sent thy Son, our Saviour, Jesus Christ, to take upon him our flesh, and to suffer death upon the cross, that all mankind should follow the example of his great humility: Mercifully grant, that we may follow the example of his patience and also be made partakers of his resurrection; through the same Jesus Christ our Lord. Amen.

Sunday

Epistle: Philippians 2.5-11   *Gospel:* Matthew 27.1-54

Monday

Lesson: Isaiah 63   *Gospel*: Mark 14

Tuesday

Lesson: Isaiah 50.5-11   *Gospel:* Mark 15.1-39

Wednesday

Epistle: Hebrews 9.16-28   *Gospel:* Luke 22

Thursday

Epistle: I Corinthians 11.17-34   *Gospel:* Luke 23.1-49

Eternal and everblessed God, you sent your Son Jesus into the world to be an example to us. Help us ever to walk in his steps.

58

Help us to walk
  In his humility,
     So that we too may be among our fellow men
     and women as those who serve;

  In his forgiveness,
     So that we too may forgive, as we hope to be for-
     given;
Help us to walk
  In his courage,
     So that nothing may ever deflect us from the way
     we ought to take;

  In his endurance,
     So that nothing may daunt or discourage us, until
     we reach our goal;

  In his loyalty,
     So that nothing may ever seduce our hearts from
     our devotion to him.

Help us to share the life that our Lord once lived on earth
that we may also share the life he lives in his risen power.

   Grant that it may be our meat and drink to do the will
   of our Father who is in heaven.

   Grant unto us to take up whatever cross is laid upon
   us and gallantly and gladly to carry it.

   Grant that
     As we may share his cross,
     So we may share his crown;
     As we share his death,
     So we may also share his life.

And so grant that having suffered with him we may also
reign with him.

This we ask for your love's sake. Amen.

Good Friday

Almighty God, we beseech thee graciously to behold this thy family, for which our Lord Jesus Christ was contented to be betrayed, and given up into the hands of wicked men, and to suffer death upon the cross, who now liveth and reigneth with thee and the Holy Ghost, ever one God, world without end. Amen.

O God of love, we remember today all that our blessed Lord endured for us.

> Let us remember how Jesus was betrayed, and given up into the hands of wicked men.

Lord Jesus, we remember today that it was one of your own familiar friends who betrayed you, and we know that there is nothing which so breaks the heart as the disloyalty of one whom we called friend. Grant that we may not betray you. Save us,

> From the cowardice,
>> which would disown you when it is hard to be true to you;
> From the disloyalty,
>> which betrays you in the hour when you need some one to stand by you;
> From the fickleness,
>> which blows hot and cold in its devotion;
> From the fair-weather friendship,
>> which, when things are difficult or dangerous,
>>> makes us ashamed to show whose we are and whom we serve.

Let us remember how Jesus suffered death upon the Cross.

Lord Jesus, help us to remember
The lengths to which your love was ready to go;
That having loved your own you loved them to the very end;
The love than which none can be greater, the love which lays down its life for its friends;
That it was while we were yet enemies that you died for us.

Let us remember how Jesus now lives and reigns.

Help us to remember
That the Crucified Lord is the Risen Lord;
That the Cross has become the Crown.

So grant unto us,
To trust in his love;
To live in his presence;
That we may share in his glory.

This we ask for your love's sake. Amen

2

*Almighty and everlasting God, by whose Spirit the whole
body of the Church is governed and sanctified: Receive our
supplications and prayers, which we offer before thee for all
estates of men in thy holy Church, that every member of the
same, in his vocation and ministry, may truly and godly
serve thee; through our Lord and Saviour Jesus Christ.*
Amen.

Lord Jesus, King and Head of the Church, today we ask you
to bless all those who do any work within your Church.

Those who preach,
  that they may have,
    your truth in their minds;
    your love in their hearts;
    your eloquence on their lips.

Those who teach,
  that they themselves may know as Saviour and Lord
    that Jesus whom they seek to introduce to others.

Those who are leaders of the youth organizations,
  that they may attract others to you
    by the strength and beauty of their own lives.

Those who serve on the Church's committees and lead
in the Church's organizations, societies and activities,
  that they may hold back none of their talents,
    and that they may allow nothing to disturb their
    fellowship.

Those who sing and those who make music,
that their praise may come from hearts that love you,
so that their work may not be a performance but
an act of worship.

Those whose duty it is to administer the affairs of the
Church,
that they may faithfully, wisely and lovingly
care for the things of your house and your household.

Those whose task it is to keep clean and fresh and tidy
the church and its premises,
that they may find joy even in these common tasks;
and make others thoughtful enough not to make the
work of all such harder than it need be.

All who come to worship and to learn each Sunday,
and to be happy in fellowship in the days of the week;
and grant that every congregation of Christian people
may be a place where people find each other and find
you.

All this we ask for your love's sake. Amen.

3

O merciful God, who hast made all men, and who hatest nothing that thou hast made, nor wouldest the death of a sinner, but rather that he should be converted and live: Have mercy upon all Jews, Turks, Infidels, and Hereticks, and take from them all ignorance, hardness of heart, and contempt of thy Word; and so fetch them home, blessed Lord, to thy flock, that they may be saved among the remnant of the true Israelites, and be made one fold under one shepherd, Jesus Christ our Lord, who liveth and reigneth with thee and the Holy Spirit, one God, world without end. Amen.

Epistle: Hebrews 10.1-25   *Gospel:* John 19.1-37

O God, you are the Father of all, and so you can never be content until all your children come home to you, and until your family is complete. We ask you to put into our hearts your own concern for those who still do not know you and love you.

Give us patience and skill,
to appeal to those whose hearts are hard, and whose minds are shut.

Give us wisdom and understanding,
to enlighten those who do not know the truth.

Help us to prove
the worth, the value, the power of your word to those who despise it, not only by the arguments of our

words but by the quality of our life. Help us so to live that they will be compelled to see that we have a secret they do not possess.

Fill us with missionary desire to win those who have never heard the message of the Christian faith, and give us such a grasp of the truth, and such a skill to commend it and defend it, that we may be able to counsel, convince and persuade those who have refused it or misunderstood it or perverted it.

So grant that the day may quickly come when everyone will be united in the one family of which you are the Head and in the one flock of which Jesus Christ is the Chief Shepherd, the day when the knowledge of you shall cover the earth as the waters cover the sea, the day when everyone shall know you and love you from the least to the greatest, the day when the kingdoms of the world will be the Kingdom of the Lord; through Jesus Christ our Lord. Amen.

Easter Even

Grant, O Lord, that as we are baptized into the death of thy blessed Son our Saviour Jesus Christ, so by continual mortifying our corrupt affections we may be buried with him; and that through the grave, and gate of death, we may pass to our joyful resurrection; for his merits, who died, and was buried, and rose again for us, thy Son Jesus Christ our Lord. Amen.

Epistle: I Peter 3.17-22   *Gospel:* Matthew 27.57-66

O God, grant to us to share in the life and the death and the resurrection of our Lord Jesus Christ.

> Grant that through him and with him we may die to sin and live to righteousness.
>
> Grant that through him and with him our old self may die, and a new self, victorious over sin and lovely with goodness, may be created.
>
> Grant that through him and with him we may become a new creation in which the old things have passed away, and in which everything has become new.

So grant that even here and now we may die to sin and be reborn to goodness.

And grant that we may be so one with our risen Lord that, when life ends for us in this world, we may know that death is the gateway to eternal life.

> Make us quite certain that those who die will live again.

Deliver us from the fear of death; and make us to know that death is not the end but the beginning of life, not the twilight but the dawn, not the midnight but the breaking day.

So grant us the certainty that beyond death there is a life,

Where the broken things are mended,
　　And the lost things found;
Where there is rest for the weary,
　　And joy for the sad;
Where all we have hoped and willed of good
　　Shall exist;
Where the dream will come true,
　　And the ideal will be realized;
Where we shall be for ever with our Lord.

So grant us the Easter certainty that life is stronger than death; through Jesus Christ our Lord. Amen.

Easter Day

Almighty God, who through thine only-begotten Son Jesus Christ hast overcome death, and opened unto us the gate of everlasting life: we humbly beseech thee, that, as by thy special grace preventing us thou dost put into our minds good desires, so by thy continual help we may bring the same to good effect; through Jesus Christ our Lord, who liveth and reigneth with thee and the Holy Ghost, ever one God, world without end. Amen.

Epistle: Colossians 3.1-7   *Gospel:* John 20.1-10

O God, our Father, you have put immortal longings into human hearts, and we thank you for them.

> For the ideals which haunt us;
> For the noble desires which move us to long for goodness;
> For the high ambitions to make life a shining thing:
> > We thank you, O God.

Forgive us, O God, for everything that keeps us from making the ideal into the real.

> For the laziness that will not make an effort;
> For the idleness which loves to do nothing;
> For the procrastination which puts things off until it is too late ever to do them;
> For the lack of perseverance which gives up too easily and too soon:
> > Forgive us, O God.

Grant unto us, God, all that we need to make the dream come true.

> Strength of will;
> Steadiness of purpose;
> Ability to do;
> Willingness to bear:
> > Grant us this, O God.
>
> Wisdom to see what we ought to do;
> Courage to begin it;
> Fidelity to continue it;
> Strength and skill to complete it:
> > Grant us this, O God.

And even if we begin and fail, help us to know that it is better to attempt and to fail in some great thing rather than not to try at all.

So grant unto us the vision, and the power to make the vision into a deed; through Jesus Christ our Lord. Amen.

Monday and Tuesday in Easter Week

Almighty God, who through thy only-begotten Son Jesus Christ hast overcome death, and opened unto us the gate of everlasting life: We humbly beseech thee, that, as by thy special grace preventing us thou dost put into our minds good desires, so by thy continual help we may bring the same to good effect; through Jesus Christ our Lord, who liveth and reigneth with thee and the Holy Ghost, ever one God, world without end. Amen.

Monday

Lesson: Acts 10.34-43   *Gospel:* Luke 24.13-35

Tuesday

Lesson: Acts 13.26-41   *Gospel:* Luke 24.36-48

O God, our Father, at Easter time we remember the great hope of eternal life which you have set before us, and we feel within our hearts the longings for goodness and for you. Grant that nothing may hinder the hope of eternal life from coming true, and the desire for goodness and for you from being realized.

Grant, O God,
    That we may never lose the way through our self-will,
        and so end up in the far countries of the soul;
    That we may never abandon the struggle,
      but that we may endure to the end,
      and so be saved;

That we may never drop out of the race,
    but that we may ever press forward
    to the goal of our high calling;
That we may never choose the cheap and passing
things,
    and let go the precious things that last for ever;
That we may never take the easy way,
    and so leave the right way;
That we may never forget
    that sweat is the price of all things,
    and that without the cross, there cannot be the
    crown.

So keep us and strengthen us by your grace that no disobedi-
ence and no weakness and no failure may stop us from
entering into the blessedness which awaits those who are
faithful in all the changes and the chances of life down even
to the gates of death; through Jesus Christ our Lord. Amen.

The First Sunday after Easter

Almighty Father, who hast given thine only Son to die for our sins, and to rise again for our justification: Grant us so to put away the leaven of malice and wickedness, that we may alway serve thee in pureness of living and truth; through the merits of the same thy Son Jesus Christ our Lord. Amen.

Epistle: I John 5.4-12   *Gospel:* John 20.19-23

O God, our Father, in the life and death and resurrection of Jesus you have given us the remedy for sin. In him you have opened to us the way to forgiveness for all our past sins, and you have given us the strength and the power to live in purity and in truth.

Help us to put away all evil things.
    Silence the evil word;
    Forbid the evil deed;
    Break the evil habit;
    Banish the evil thought;
    Take away the evil desire and the evil ambition;
        and make our lives to shine like lights
        in this dark world.

Help us to live in purity.
    Make all our words so pure
        that you may hear them;
    Make all our deeds so pure
        that you may see them;

Make all our thoughts and desires so pure
    that they may bear your scrutiny.
And so grant that we being pure in heart
    may see you.

Help us to live in truth.
    Grant
        That we may never speak or act a lie;
        That we may never be misled by false or mistaken
        beliefs;
        That we may never evade the truth,
            even when we do not want to see it.

    Grant to us at all times
        To seek and to find;
        To know and to love;
        To obey and to live
            the truth.

This we ask for the sake of him who is the Way, the Truth
and the Life, even for the sake of Jesus Christ our Lord.
Amen.

Almighty God, who hast given thine only Son, to be unto us both a sacrifice for sin, and also an ensample of godly life: Give us grace that we may always most thankfully receive that his inestimable benefit, and also daily endeavour ourselves to follow the blessed steps of his most holy life; through the same Jesus Christ our Lord. Amen.

Epistle: I Peter 2.19-25   *Gospel:* John 10.11-16

O God, our Father, we thank you for Jesus Christ, your Son, our Lord.

> We thank you for his sacrifice for us.
>> That he gave his life a ransom for many;
>> That he was obedient unto death, even the death of the Cross;
>>> We thank you, O God.

> We thank you for his example to us.
>> That he left us an example that we should follow in his steps;
>> That he is to us the Way, the Truth and the Life;
>> That in him you have shown us what is good:
>>> We thank you, O God.

Help us to follow the example he has given us.

> <u>Help us to follow the example,</u>
>> Of his courage,
>>> that nothing may deflect us from the way we ought to take;

74

Of his humility,
   that in us too self may die;
Of his obedience,
   that for us too to do your will may be life itself;
Of his kindness,
   that we too may go about doing good;
Of his forgiveness,
   that we too may be tender-hearted, forgiving one
      another, even as you for his sake have forgiven
      us;
Of his love,
   that the last particle of hatred may be banished
      from our hearts and from our lives.

So grant that we may show that we are redeemed, so that others may believe in our redeemer; through Jesus Christ our Lord. Amen.

The Third Sunday after Easter

Almighty God, who showest to them that be in error the light of thy truth, to the intent that they may return into the way of righteousness: Grant unto all them that are admitted into the fellowship of Christ's Religion, that they may eschew those things which are contrary to their profession, and follow all such things as are agreeable to the same; through our Lord Jesus Christ. Amen.

Epistle: I Peter 2.11-17   *The Gospel:* John 16.16-22

O God, help us at all times to make our deeds fit our words, and to make our conduct match our profession; and grant that we may never say one thing with our lips and another with our lives.

Grant that we may not praise service and practise selfishness.

Grant that for us sympathy may never only be a thing of the emotions, but that it may always issue in action to help. Grant that, when we feel sorry for some one, we may not be satisfied until we have done something to help.

Grant that we may not praise love and practise bitterness.

Grant that we may not sing of the beauty of loving one another, and yet refuse to forgive one another. Grant that we may not dream of a time of brotherly love, and yet be unable to live at peace with our neighbour.

76

Grant that we may not praise honesty and practise falsehood.

Grant that we may not be guilty of the hypocrisy which says one thing with its lips and means another in its heart, and which is one thing to a person's face and another behind his back. Grant that we may not pay lip service to the truth, and yet be willing to evade, suppress, or twist the truth, when we think that it suits us to do so.

Grant that we may not praise generosity and practise meanness.

Keep us from the hypocrisy of singing hymns about giving everything to you, and then grudging every penny we give and every hour we devote to the service of your people and your Church.

Keep us, O God, from bringing discredit by our life and our actions, our words and our behaviour on the faith which we profess, the Church to which we belong, and the Master whom we ought to serve; through Jesus Christ our Lord. Amen.

O Almighty God, who alone canst order the unruly wills and affections of sinful men: Grant unto thy people, that they may love the things which thou commandest, and desire that which thou dost promise; that so, among the sundry and manifold changes of the world, our hearts may surely there be fixed, where true joys are to be found; through Jesus Christ our Lord. Amen.

Epistle: James 1.17-21   *Gospel:* John 16.5-15

O God, our Father, you gave us wills of our own that we should make them yours. And yet there is in us a pride, a self-will, a stubbornness, which make us impatient of all control and determined on our own way.

Help us, O God, to remember what you are.
    Help us to remember
    Your wisdom,
        that we may never doubt,
            that you know best.

Help us to remember
    Your love,
        that we may never doubt
            that you will seek only our good.

Help us to remember
    Your power,
        that we may never doubt,
            that you can do all that you promise.

Grant that we may willingly and gladly obey you.
Grant that we may seek,
Only to do your will;
Only to gladden your love;
Only to seek the rewards which you alone can give.

To that end take from us,
The pride,
which will not surrender its will to you;
The blindness,
which does not see the wonder of your love;
The short sight,
which seizes the pleasure of a moment,
and forfeits the eternal joy.

So grant that in your service we may find our perfect freedom, and in doing your will our peace; through Jesus Christ our Lord. Amen.

The Fifth Sunday after Easter

O Lord, from whom all good things do come: Grant to us thy humble servants, that by thy holy inspiration we may think those things that be good, and by thy merciful guiding may perform the same; through Jesus Christ our Lord. Amen.

Epistle: James 1.22-27   *Gospel:* John 16.23-33

O God, without you we can neither think nor act aright.

Help us to banish from our minds,
> All bitter thoughts,
>> which would divide us from others;
>
> All proud thoughts,
>> which would make us conceited and contemptuous of others,
>>
>>> and which would make us think of our own place and prestige;
>
> All selfish thoughts,
>> which would make us regardless of the needs and of the feelings of others;
>
> All impure thoughts,
>> which would give temptation its chance,
>>> and which would leave a stain upon our minds.

Help us to banish from our lives,
> All careless work,
>> which is not good enough to show to you;
>
> All cowardly action,
>> which is afraid to show what it believes;

80

All thoughtless action,
    which forgets to look at the consequences of what it
    does;
All rash action,
    which is at the mercy of the impulse or the passion
    of the moment.
Help us to think
    In purity and in love;
Help us to act
    In honesty and honour.

Hear this our prayer; through Jesus Christ our Lord. Amen.

Ascension Day

Grant, we beseech thee, Almighty God, that like as we do believe thy only-begotten Son our Lord Jesus Christ to have ascended into the heavens; so we may also in heart and mind thither ascend, and with him continually dwell, who liveth and reigneth with thee and the Holy Ghost, one God, world without end. Amen.

Lesson: Acts 1.1-11   *Gospel:* Mark 16.14-20

Eternal God, as today we remember that our Blessed Lord ascended up into heaven, help us to set our affections on the things that are above.

Grant that your voice may speak to us
more compellingly than any earthly voice;
Grant that your will may be dearer to us
than any earthly desires;
Grant that your purpose may mean more to us
than any earthly ambition.
Help us to judge things,
not in the light of time,
but in the light of eternity.
Help us to value things,
not as men and women value them,
but as you value them;
and so to see that it will profit us nothing
to gain the whole world,
if in so doing we lose our soul.

82

Help us to see things,
  not as men and women see them,
  but as you see them;
  so that we may see
  what things are important,
  and what things do not matter,
  even if the world holds them dear.

Help us to act,
  not for human pleasure,
  but to please you.
Help us to walk,
  not looking for human favour,
  but with our eyes steadfastly fixed on Jesus.

So grant that in the here and now we may always be conscious of the there and then, and that here in the present we may ever remember the things which are beyond; through Jesus Christ our Lord. Amen.

Sunday after Ascension Day

O God, the King of glory, who hast exalted thine only Son Jesus Christ with great triumph unto thy kingdom in heaven: We beseech thee, leave us not comfortless; but send to us thine Holy Ghost to comfort us, and exalt us unto the same place whither our Saviour Christ is gone before, who liveth and reigneth with thee and the Holy Ghost, one God, world without end. Amen.

Epistle: I Peter 4.7-11   *Gospel:* John 15.26-16.4

O God, our Father, we remember that Jesus promised that he would send to us the Holy Spirit from you. Keep that promise to us today.

He called his Spirit the Spirit of truth.

Open our eyes that we may see the truth;

Strengthen our hearts that we may face the truth;

Enlighten our minds that we may understand the truth;

Make our memories retentive that we may remember the truth;

Make resolute our wills that we may obey the truth, through the Spirit which he has promised to us.

He said that the Spirit would bring to our remembrance all that he had said.

O God, when we are in danger of forgetting the things which we should always remember, grant that your Spirit may bring again to our memory the promises, the commands and the presence of our risen and blessed Lord.

He said that the Spirit would take what is his and declare it to us.

O God, when we do not know what to do, when we find the teachings of our Lord either difficult to understand or to apply, grant that your Spirit may show us what to believe and what to do.

He said that the Spirit would tell us things which in the days of his flesh he could not say to his disciples, because they were not ready to receive them.

O God, keep us from ever thinking of our Christian faith and belief as something static. Help us to remember that there are ever new depths of truth, new vistas of beauty, new glories of experience, new gifts of power into which the Spirit can lead us.

He said that the Spirit would lead us into all truth.

Help us to remember that all truth belongs to you—
> The skill of the scientist and the thought of the philosopher;
> The inspiration of the poet, the vision of the artist, the melody of the musician;
> The craft of the craftsman and the strength of body and of mind by which we make a living.

And since everything comes from you, help us to use everything for you and for our fellow men and women; through Jesus Christ our Lord. Amen.

Whitsunday and Monday and Tuesday in Whitsun Week

God, who as at this time didst teach the hearts of thy faithful people, by the sending to them the light of thy Holy Spirit: Grant us by the same Spirit to have a right judgement in all things, and evermore to rejoice in his holy comfort; through the merits of Jesus Christ our Saviour, who liveth and reigneth with thee, in the unity of the same Spirit, one God, world without end. Amen.

Whitsunday

Lesson: Acts 2.1-11   *Gospel:* John 14.15-31

Monday in Whitsun Week

Lesson: Acts 10.34-48   *Gospel:* John 3.16-21

Tuesday in Whitsun Week

Lesson: Acts 8.14-17   *Gospel:* John 10. 1-10

O God, our Father, give us your Holy Spirit in our hearts and in our minds that we may ever choose aright.

> Give us your Holy Spirit that we may know,
> > which way to choose, and which way to refuse;
> > which choice to make, and which choice to reject;
> > which course of action to take, and which course of action to avoid.

> Give us your Holy Spirit,
> > to enlighten our minds,
> > > to see what we ought to do;

to strengthen our wills,
to choose the right course of action,
and to abide by it;
to empower our lives,
to follow the right way to the end.

Give us your Holy Spirit,
to cleanse our minds of all evil and impure
thoughts;
to fill our hearts with all lovely and noble desires;
to make our lives
wise with knowledge,
beautiful with love,
useful with service.

Give us your Holy Spirit,
to light up the pages of your Book for us;
to teach us for what we ought to pray;
to enrich our lives with the fruit which only he can
give.

Grant us all this for your love's sake. Amen.

Trinity Sunday

Almighty and everlasting God, who hast given unto us thy servants grace by the confession of a true faith to acknowledge the glory of the eternal Trinity, and in the power of the Divine Majesty to worship the Unity: We beseech thee, that thou wouldest keep us stedfast in this faith, and evermore defend us from all adversities, who livest and reignest, one God, world without end. Amen.

Lesson: Revelation 4.1-11   *Gospel:* John 3.1-14

Let us remember God in Creation

O God, the Father, we thank you for your creating power.

> That you have made all things and made them well;
> That you have given us all things richly to enjoy;
> For the beauty and the bounty of this fair earth;
> And for the creating power which can make all things new:
>> We thank you, O Father.

> Forgive us if in pride and selfishness and in anger we have misused your gifts, and have used for death that which was meant for life.

Let us remember God in Redemption

O Lord Jesus Christ the Son, we thank you for your redeeming power.

> That you loved us and gave yourself for us;
> That you gave your life a ransom for many, a ransom for us;

That you were obedient unto death, even the death of the Cross:

> We thank you, O Christ.

Forgive us if we have treated your love lightly as a little thing, and if we have never even begun to love you as you have first loved us.

Let us remember God in Providence

O Holy Spirit of God, we thank you for your keeping power.

For the guidance you have given us;
For the knowledge you have brought us;
For your continual upholding, strengthening, protecting power:

> We thank you, O Spirit of God.

Forgive us if we have tried to live life alone, and have despoiled ourselves of the divine help we might have had from you.

And may the blessing of God, the Father, the Son, and the Holy Spirit, the Three in One, and the One in Three, be on us now and stay with each one of us always. Amen.

The First Sunday after Trinity

O God, the strength of all them that put their trust in thee: Mercifully accept our prayers; and because through the weakness of our mortal nature we can do no good thing without thee, grant us the help of thy grace, that in keeping of thy commandments we may please thee, both in will and deed; through Jesus Christ our Lord. Amen.

Epistle: I John 4.7-21　　　　　　*Gospel:* Luke 16.19-31

O God, our Father, we know our own weakness.

Our wills are weak.
We know the right, and cannot do it.
We make our resolutions, and cannot keep them.
We see the ideal,
but the byways are so fascinating,
the uphill road is so difficult,
that we lose the way.

Our passions are so strong.
Our emotions are stronger than our wills.
We are swept away by the passion of the moment.
The sudden impulse will brook no denial.
And we do,
what we never meant to do,
and what we regret doing.

We need your grace,
Grace to overcome evil and to do the right,
Grace to rid of ourselves of old faults, and to gain
new virtues,

90

Grace,
> To turn the vision into the deed,
> To turn the ideal into the real,
> To turn the dream into the action,
> To do that which we already know we ought to do.

So grant that your grace may make our weakness strong,
> So that we may overcome all evil,
> So that without stumbling and without straying
> we may walk stedfastly in the way everlasting,
> So that we may obey your commandments,
> So that we may at the last reach our journey's end in
> honour and hear you say: Well done!

Hear this our prayer; through Jesus Christ our Lord. Amen.

The Second Sunday after Trinity

O Lord, who never failest to help and govern them whom thou dost bring up in thy stedfast fear and love: Keep us, we beseech thee, under the protection of thy good providence, and make us to have a perpetual fear and love of thy holy Name; through Jesus Christ our Lord. Amen.

Epistle: I John 3.13-24   *Gospel:* Luke 14.16-24

Keep us, O God, for ever in your fear and in your love.

    Grant us that godly fear,
        which will keep us from breaking your commandments;
        which will keep us from disobeying your law;
        which will keep us from refusing your guidance.
    Grant us that godly fear,
        which will keep us from hurting others;
        which will keep us from shaming ourselves;
        which will keep us from being untrue to you.
    Grant us that love of you,
        which will keep us from grieving your heart;
        which will keep us from frustrating your purposes;
        which will keep us from disappointing your hopes.
    Grant us that love of you,
        which will make us love you,
          as you have first loved us;
        which will make us love our fellow men and women,
          as you have loved them;
        which will make us give ourselves for him,
          who loved us and gave himself for us.

So grant that,
    fearing you and loving you,
        we may be safe from sin,
        and strong in devotion;

            through Jesus Christ our Lord. Amen.

The Third Sunday after Trinity

O Lord, we beseech thee mercifully to hear us; and grant that we, to whom thou hast given an hearty desire to pray, may by thy mighty aid be defended and comforted in all dangers and adversities; through Jesus Christ our Lord. Amen.

Epistle: I Peter 5.5-11　　　　　　*Gospel:* Luke 15.1-10

O God, our Father, we thank you that you have put into our hearts the desire to pray. We thank you that you have made us such that in any time of trouble we instinctively turn to you.

We thank you that you have given us the gift of prayer,
　　　that your ear is ever listening
　　　　　to catch our every word,
　　　　　　　and to hear even the heart's unspoken cry for help;
　　　that the door to your presence
　　　　　is never shut,
　　　　　　　to those who seek to enter on their knees.

We thank you that you have given us the confidence to pray. We thank you that you have told us,
　　　that you are our Father,
　　　that your name is love;
　　　that you love each one of us,
　　　　　as if there was only one of us to love,
　　　　　　　and that no child of yours can be lost in the crowd.

We thank you that you have given us
    unanswerable proof of your love,
        by sending your Son Jesus Christ,
            to live, to suffer and to die for us.

Give us now an answer to our prayers.
    We do not ask that we should be protected from all
    pain and sorrow, from all danger and distress. We ask
    for humility to accept whatever comes to us, and for
    courage, and fortitude and endurance to come safely
    through it, and to come out on the other side finer in
    character, and nearer to you.

    We do not ask that you should answer our prayers as
    we in our ignorance would wish, but as you in your
    mercy and love know best.

        Into your hands we commend our spirits,
            because we know that
                you are love to care,
                mercy to bless,
                power to save.

Hear these our prayers for your love's sake. Amen.

The Fourth Sunday after Trinity

*O God, the protector of all that trust in thee, without whom
nothing is strong, nothing is holy: Increase and multiply
upon us thy mercy; that, thou being our ruler and guide, we
may so pass through things temporal, that we finally lose
not the things eternal: Grant this, O heavenly Father, for
Jesus Christ's sake our Lord.* Amen.

Epistle: Romans 8.18-23   *Gospel:* Luke 6.36-42

O God, you are our refuge and strength, and without you
we can do nothing.

> Unless you strengthen us,
>> We cannot bear our burdens;
>> We cannot face our responsibilities;
>> We cannot stand the strain and the tension of life.

> Unless you guide us,
>> We cannot make the right decisions;
>> We cannot find the right way;
>> We cannot bring life in safety to its journey's end.

O God, our Father, you are the Holy One and the Source
of all goodness and without you we cannot live aright.

> Unless you cleanse us,
>> We cannot conquer our temptations;
>> We cannot tame our passions;
>> We cannot master our desires.

Unless you control us,
    We cannot guard our thoughts;
    We cannot discipline our speech;
    We cannot do only the things which are right.

O God, help us to submit to you, that you may strengthen us and guide us, that you may cleanse us and control us, that you may be our Ruler and our Guide, so that all through life we may walk in the way everlasting and finally enter without shame into your presence; through Jesus Christ our Lord. Amen.

The Fifth Sunday after Trinity

Grant, O Lord, we beseech thee, that the course of this world may be so peaceably ordered by thy governance, that thy Church may joyfully serve thee in all godly quietness; through Jesus Christ our Lord. Amen.

Epistle: I Peter 3.8-15   *Gospel:* Luke 5.1-11

O God, Ruler of all, grant that the state of the world may be such that everywhere doors may open for the truth of your word and the saving power of your gospel to spread unhindered throughout it.

Take from the world all threats of war. Enable the nations to live in brotherhood together. Teach us to direct the powers which you have given us not to the destroying but to the saving of life. Make us know that this is one world, and that those who are in it must be one.

Take from the world all religious intolerance. Help all people to remember that there are more ways than one to you, and that you have your own secret stairway into every heart. Grant that we may not brand as heretics all who do not think as we do.

Take from the Church its divisions. Bring quickly the time when indeed there will be one flock and one shepherd. Help us to think far more of the Christ who unites, and far less of the systems which divide.

Take from all lands all enmity between class and class and party and party. Help all people to see beyond their individual interests to the common good.

Take from the world all enmity and suspicion between nation and nation, between race and race, between colour and colour. Help them to find a new fellowship which will transcend colour and country, and which will make them one family in you.

Take from the world all injustice and all poverty and make it a world where poverty shall cease to fester and where none shall prey on any other.

Hear these our prayers, and inspire us by your Spirit and strengthen us by your grace to build the kind of world this world ought to be through Jesus Christ our Lord. Amen.

O God, who hast prepared for them that love thee such good things as pass man's understanding: Pour into our hearts such love toward thee, that we, loving thee above all things, may obtain thy promises, which exceed all that we can desire; through Jesus Christ our Lord. Amen.

Epistle: Romans 6.3-11   *Gospel:* Matthew 5.20-26

O God, our Father, you have loved us with an everlasting love, and in your mercy you have great rewards for those who are loyal to you. Help us so to live that we shall one day enter into these things which you have promised to your faithful servants.

> Give us such a love of you,
>> that we may find obedience,
>>> not a burden but a delight;
>> that we may find the cost of loyalty,
>>> not a trial but a privilege;
>> that we may find your law,
>>> not a chain to bind us,
>>> but wings to uplift us.

> Give us such a love of others,
>> that we may find service,
>>> not wearisome but joyous;
>> that we may find giving,
>>> not a pain but a pleasure;
>> that we may find sharing,
>>> not a duty but a joy.

100

Give us such a love of your Church,
    that we may find its worship,
        not a dead convention,
        but a living thrill;
    that we may find the obligations of church member-
    ship,
        not something to resent,
        but something in which to rejoice;
    that we may find work within it,
        not an imposition,
        but an opportunity.

So grant that love
  may sweeten all obedience,
  and lighten every task,

so that living for you, for our fellow men and women, and for your Church may be all joy; through Jesus Christ our Lord. Amen.

The Seventh Sunday after Trinity

Lord of all power and might, who art the author and giver of all good things: Graft in our hearts the love of thy Name, increase in us true religion, nourish us with all goodness, and of thy great mercy keep us in the same; through Jesus Christ our Lord. Amen.

Epistle: Romans 6.19-23   *Gospel:* Mark 8.1-10

O God, our Father, Giver of every good and perfect gift,

> Give us in our living true love of you.
> Give us the love,
> > which will grudge no gift,
> > which will refuse no obedience,
> > which will resent no trial.
>
> Give us in our living true religion.
> Help us,
> > to show our love for you
> > > by loving others;
> > to be in the world,
> > > and yet to keep our garments
> > > unspotted by the world;
> > to make the deeds of our hands
> > > match the words of our lips.
>
> Give us in our living true goodness.
> Give us the goodness,
> > which is not only pure,
> > > but also lovely;

which does not sin itself,
  but which loves the sinner;
which has upon it the reflection
  of the loveliness of the life of Jesus.

Give us in our living the gift of perseverance.
  When we have chosen our way,
    help us never to stray from it;
  when we fall,
    help us always to rise again;
  when there is a cross to bear,
    help us to see beyond it the crown.

So help us to live life
    in love, in service, and in fidelity,
    that we may come to the end in peace,
    and enter into blessedness;
        through Jesus Christ our Lord. Amen.

The Eighth Sunday after Trinity

O God, whose never-failing providence ordereth all things both in heaven and earth: We humbly beseech thee to put away from us all hurtful things, and to give us those things which be profitable for us; through Jesus Christ our Lord. Amen.

Epistle: Romans 8.12-17   *Gospel:* Matthew 7.15-21

O God, our Father, we know that the issues of life and death are in your hands, and we know that you are loving us with an everlasting love. If it is your will, grant to us to live in happiness and in peace.

In all our undertakings,
> Grant us prosperity and good success.

In all our friendships,
> Grant us to find our friends faithful and true.

In all bodily things,
> Make us fit and healthy,
>> Able for the work of the day.

In all the things of the mind,
> Make us calm and serene,
>> Free from anxiety and worry.

In material things,
> Save us from poverty and from want.

In spiritual things,
> Save us from doubt and from distrust.

Grant us
    In our work satisfaction;
    In our study true wisdom;
    In our pleasure gladness;
    In our love loyalty.

And if misfortune does come to us, grant that any trial may only bring us closer to one another and closer to you; and grant that nothing may shake our certainty that you work all things together for good, and that a Father's hand will never cause his child a needless tear.

Hear this our prayer; through Jesus Christ our Lord. Amen.

The Ninth Sunday after Trinity

Grant to us, Lord, we beseech thee, the spirit to think and do always such things as be rightful; that we, who cannot do anything that is good without thee, may by thee be enabled to live according to thy will; through Jesus Christ our Lord. Amen.

Epistle: I Corinthians 10.1-13   *Gospel:* Luke 16.1-9

O God, our Father, we know our own weakness and we know your power. And this day we take

> Our helplessness to your strength;
> Our ignorance to your wisdom;
> Our sin to your purity;
> Our need to your love.

We cannot decide aright what we should do;
> Grant us the guidance which will save us from all mistakes.

We cannot conquer our temptations;
> Grant us the grace which can make us clean and keep us clean.

We cannot bear the toil of life;
> Grant us the strength to pass the breaking-point and not to break.

We cannot escape the worry of life;
> Grant us the peace that passes understanding,
>   which the world cannot give or ever take away.

We cannot face the responsibilities of life;
  Grant us to know that there is nothing that we have to
  face alone.

We cannot solve the problems of life;
  Grant us in your wisdom to find the answers
    to the questions which perplex our ignorance.

We cannot find the right way;
  Grant that at every cross-roads of life
    your Spirit may be there to direct us.

We cannot face life alone;
  Grant us to remember that our Lord is with us always
    to the end of the world and beyond.

We cannot face death alone;
  Grant us to be very sure that nothing in life or in death,
    can separate us from your love in Christ Jesus our
    Lord.

We come to you for strength in life and for hope when life is
ended; through Jesus Christ our Lord. Amen.

The Tenth Sunday after Trinity

Let thy merciful ears, O Lord, be open to the prayers of thy humble servants; and that they may obtain their petitions make them to ask such things as shall please thee; through Jesus Christ our Lord. Amen.

Epistle: I Corinthians 12.1-11   *Gospel:* Luke 19.41-47a

O God, our Father, help us only to desire in our hearts and only to ask in our prayers the things which please you.

Help us to ask that we may learn,
    not how to get our own way,
        but how to take your way;
    not how to do what we want,
        but how to do what you want.

Help us to ask that we may learn,
    not how to grow rich in this world's goods,
        but how to lay up treasure in heaven;
    not how to realize our dreams of worldly greatness
        but how to live in humble service.

Help us to ask that we may learn,
    not how to live in the independence of pride,
        but in dependence on you;
    not how to know and plan the future,
        but how to take one step at a time,
            our hand in yours.

Help us to ask that we may learn,
 not how to gratify,
  but how to master our desires;
 not how to satisfy,
  but how to tame our passions.

Help us to ask that we may learn,
 not how to live as if this world were all,
  but how to live
  as pilgrims of eternity,
  who have here no abiding city,
  but who are on the way to that city,
  whose maker and builder you are;
 not how to please ourselves in this world,
  but how to meet your judgment,
  when this world is ended.

Hear these our prayers; through Jesus Christ our Lord.
Amen.

The Eleventh Sunday after Trinity

O God, who declarest thy almighty power most chiefly in shewing mercy and pity: Mercifully grant unto us such a measure of thy grace, that we, running the way of thy commandments, may obtain thy gracious promises, and be made partakers of thy heavenly treasure; through Jesus Christ our Lord. Amen.

Epistle: I Corinthians 15.1-11   *Gospel:* Luke 18.9-14

O God, our Father, we come to you,

> Not because we are strong,
> but because we are weak;
> Not because we have any merits of our own,
> but because we need mercy and help.

Grant unto us this day the mercy and the pity which are yours.

Give us grace,

> Always to keep your commandments;
> Always to accept your guidance;
> Always to obey your word;
> Never to leave your path,
> but always to walk in the way everlasting.

Give us grace,

> So to run,
> that we may reach our goal;

So to fight,
    that we may win the victor's crown;
So to keep the faith,
    that to the very end we may be true.

Give us grace so to live in time that we may receive the true
treasure in eternity.

Help us to be,
    So pure in heart,
        that we may see you;
    So faithful unto death,
        that we may receive the crown of life;
    So close to you in our walk upon earth,
        that, when earth is ended,
            we may be for ever with our Lord.

In your mercy and pity,
    Make our ignorance wise with your wisdom;
    Make our weakness strong with your strength,
        so that our brief life may be clothed with your eternal
        life;
            through Jesus Christ our Lord. Amen.

The Twelfth Sunday after Trinity

Almighty and everlasting God, who art always more ready to hear than we to pray, and art wont to give more than either we desire, or deserve: Pour down upon us the abundance of thy mercy; forgiving us those things whereof our conscience is afraid, and giving us those good things which we are not worthy to ask, but through the merits and mediation of Jesus Christ, thy Son, our Lord. Amen.

Epistle: II Corinthians 3.4-9   *Gospel:* Mark 7.31-37

O God, our Father, we cannot doubt your generous love. We know that, if you gave us the gift of your Son, you will with him freely give us all things.

We know that, even when we sin, you still love us, and your only desire is that we should repent and come back to you. Forgive us for our sins.

> For the things which we try to hide from others;
> For the things which we try to put out of our minds and forget;
> For the things for which others find it very difficult to forgive us;
> For the things for which we cannot forgive ourselves;
> For the things which sometimes in our folly we try to hide from you:
> **Forgive us, O God.**

112

For the heartbreak and the sorrow, the worry and the
anxiety we have caused;
For any time when we made it easier for some one else
to go wrong;
For the harm that we have done, and can never now
undo:
Forgive us, O God.

Grant us the gifts which you alone can give.

Give us,
The courage to admit our mistakes;
The grace which will enable us to rise when we fall,
and to begin all over again when we fail;
The real penitence, which humbly and sincerely asks
for forgiveness, when it has done wrong.

Give us this day,
Forgiveness for the past;
Courage for the present;
Hope for the future,

And in your infinite mercy come to meet our infinite need;
through Jesus Christ our Lord. Amen.

The Thirteenth Sunday after Trinity

Almighty and merciful God, of whose only gift it cometh that thy faithful people do unto thee true and laudable service: Grant, we beseech thee, that we may so faithfully serve thee in this life, that we fail not finally to attain thy heavenly promises; through the merits of Jesus Christ our Lord. Amen.

Epistle: Galatians 3.16-22   *Gospel:* Luke 10.23-37

Eternal God, we know that in our own strength we cannot give you the service that we ought to give. So then we ask you to give us what we need to enable us to serve you more nearly as we ought.

> Give us
>> Self-discipline,
>>> so that we may choose,
>>> not what we wish but what we ought;
>>
>> Strength of will,
>>> so that we may accept the right,
>>>> however difficult it is,
>>> and refuse the wrong,
>>>> however attractive it is;
>>
>> Obedience,
>>> so that in doing your will
>>>> we may find our peace;

Trust,
    so that we may be able willingly to accept
        even that which we do not understand,
    and so that, whatever happens,
        we may never doubt your love.

In every time of decision,
    give us light to see what we ought to do,
        and give us resolution, courage and strength to
          do it;

In every time of temptation,
    give us strength to resist all evil,
        and to do the right;

In every time of effort,
    give us power to do what by ourselves we could
    not do,
        and perseverance to bring the task to its ap-
        pointed end;

In every time of sorrow,
    give us grace to remember
    that we have hopes as well as memories,
    so that we may think more of the glory of life
        eternal,
    than of the brief darkness of death.

So grant that guided and strengthened by you
    we may live in honour,
    and come to the end in peace,
    and finally enter into glory;

through Jesus Christ our Lord. Amen.

The Fourteenth Sunday after Trinity

Almighty and everlasting God, give unto us the increase of faith, hope, and charity; and, that we may obtain that which thou dost promise, make us to love that which thou dost command; through Jesus Christ our Lord. Amen.

Epistle: Galatians 5.16-24   *Gospel:* Luke 17.11-19

O God, our Father, you alone can enable us to accept and to obey your commandments and to do your will.

Increase our faith.
> Help us,
>> To trust you when the skies are dark;
>> To accept that which we cannot understand;
>> To be quite sure that all things can work together for good to those who love you.

Increase our hope.
> Give us
>> The hope which has seen things at their worst, and which refuses to despair;
>> The hope that is able to fail, and yet to try again;
>> The hope which can accept disappointment, and yet not abandon hope.

Increase our love.
> Help us,
>> To love our fellow men and women, as you love them;
>> To love you as you have first loved us;
>> To love loyalty to our Lord above all other things.

Help us so to love you that your commandments will never be a weariness and a burden to us, but that it will be a joy for us to obey them, so that in obedience to you we may find our perfect freedom, and in doing your will our peace.

So grant to us,
To fight the good fight;
To run the straight race;
To keep the faith,
    that we may win the glory and the crown.

Hear these our prayers for your love's sake. Amen.

The Fifteenth Sunday after Trinity

Keep, we beseech thee, O Lord, thy Church with thy perpetual mercy; and, because the frailty of man without thee cannot but fall, keep us ever by thy help from all things hurtful, and lead us to all things profitable to our salvation; through Jesus Christ our Lord. Amen.

Epistle: Galatians 6.11-18   *Gospel:* Matthew 6.24-34

O God, our Father, we know our own weakness.

Our minds are darkened,
and by ourselves we cannot find and know the truth.
Our wills are weak,
and by ourselves we cannot resist temptation,
or bring to its completion that which we resolve to do.
Our hearts are fickle,
and by ourselves we cannot give to you
the loyalty which is your due.
Our steps are faltering,
and by ourselves we cannot walk in your straight way.

So this day we ask you,

To enlighten us;
To strengthen us;
To guide us,

that we may know you, and love you, and follow you all the days of our life.

Give to your Church your blessing and your protection.

Guide her in her thinking,
that she may be saved from the heresies
which destroy the faith.

Strengthen her in her witness,
that she may bring no discredit on the name she
bears.

Inspire her in her fellowship,
that those who enter her may find within her
your friendship and the friendship of their fellow
men and women.

So grant that guided, strengthened, and inspired by you,
your Church may shine like a beacon of truth, of loyalty,
and of love within the darkness of the world; through Jesus
Christ our Lord. Amen.

The Sixteenth Sunday after Trinity

O Lord, we beseech thee, let thy continual pity cleanse and defend thy Church; and, because it cannot continue in safety without thy succour, preserve it evermore by thy help and goodness; through Jesus Christ our Lord. Amen.

Epistle: Ephesians 3.13-21   *Gospel:* Luke 7.11-17

O God, our Father, you intended the Church to be the Body of Jesus Christ, your Son. You meant the Church to be a voice to speak for him, hands to work for him, feet to go upon his errands; and without your help the Church can never be what you meant it to be.

We ask you to cleanse the Church.
>All bitterness that would disturb its fellowship;
>All divisions that would destroy its unity;
>All coldness that would lessen its devotion;
>All slackness that would paralyse its action:
>>Take from your Church, O God.

We ask you to defend the Church.
>From all persecution and attack from without;
>From all heresy and false doctrine from within;
>From the hostility of its enemies and the failure of its members:
>>Defend your Church, O God.

We ask you to help and to assist your Church.
Give to it
>Courage in its speaking,
>And tirelessness in its acting.

Give to it

> Ministers who are men and women,
> In whose minds there is true learning,
> On whose lips there is eloquence,
> In whose hearts there is devotion,
> Who are apt to study, skilled to teach,
> Wise to counsel, brave to act, loving to help.

Give to it

> Members who are generous in giving, faithful in prayer,
> Diligent in worship, Christlike in witness.

So grant that, preserved by your help and goodness, the Church may indeed be the Body of Jesus Christ. This we ask for your love's sake. Amen.

The Seventeenth Sunday after Trinity

Lord, we pray thee that thy grace may always prevent and follow us, and make us continually to be given to all good works; through Jesus Christ our Lord. Amen.

Epistle: Ephesians 4.1-6   *Gospel:* Luke 14.1-11

O God, our Father, we know that your grace is sufficient for all things. Give to us at all times this all-sufficient grace, that in it our weakness may be made strong, our ignorance wise, and our sins forgiven.

Let your grace go ever before us,
That we may know the way to take;
That we may see the path in which we ought to walk;
That at each cross-roads of life
we may see the road we ought to choose;
That without falling and without straying
we may in safety reach our journey's end.

Let your grace follow after us,
That we may ever be
Protected by your power,
Upheld by your kindness,
Warmed by your love.

So equip us with your grace that others may see our good works and glorify you our Father in Heaven.

By your grace make us
Firm in resolution,
Courageous in action,
Constant in devotion,

122

Unwearying in forgiveness,
Loyal in love,
Lovely in life.

So grant that guided and protected, upheld and equipped by your grace we may live

To our own honour,
In the service of our fellow men,
And to your glory.

This we ask through Jesus Christ our Lord. Amen.

The Eighteenth Sunday after Trinity

*Lord, we beseech thee, grant thy people grace to withstand
the temptations of the world, the flesh, and the devil, and
with pure hearts and minds to follow thee the only God;
through Jesus Christ our Lord.* Amen.

Epistle: I Corinthians 1.4-8   *Gospel:* Matthew 22.34-46

O God, our Father, because we are men and women with
human hearts and human minds and human emotions, there
is no escape for us from temptation.

> Defend us from the temptations of the world.
>> From lowering our standards and abandoning our
>> ideals;
>> From the cautious conformity that fears to be differ-
>> ent;
>> From the materialism which really believes that
>> human life does consist in the abundance of the
>> things we possess:
>>> Defend us, O God.
>
> Defend us from the temptations of the flesh.
>> From the passion which can wreck life;
>> From the impulses which can bring regret to follow;
>> From the too strong emotions which can sweep us to
>> disaster;
>> From the freedom which has become licence and the
>> love which has become lust:
>>> Defend us, O God.

Defend us from the temptations of the devil.
> From yielding to any seduction to sin;
> From the power of the fascination of the forbidden thing;
> From forgetting that in the end our sin
>> is bound to find us out:
>>> Defend us, O God.

Give us by your grace
> Hearts so pure that they love only the highest;
> Minds so clean that they seek only the truth.

And grant that nothing may lure us from our loyalty, and nothing deflect us from our path; and so help us all our days ever to follow you and never to turn back and never to lose our way: through Jesus Christ our Lord. Amen.

The Nineteenth Sunday after Trinity

O God, forasmuch as without thee we are not able to please thee: Mercifully grant that thy Holy Spirit may in all things direct and rule our hearts; through Jesus Christ our Lord. Amen.

Epistle: Ephesians 4.17-32   *Gospel:* Matthew 9.1-8

O God, our Father, we are helpless without your help.
    Unless you help us,
        we can see the ideal,
            but we cannot reach it;
        we can know the right,
            but we cannot do it;
        we can recognize our duty,
            but we cannot perform it;
        we can seek the truth,
            but we can never wholly find it.

All our lives we are haunted by the difference between what we ought to do and what in fact we can do.
    By your Holy Spirit,
        Enlighten our minds,
            that we may reach beyond guessing to knowing,
            and beyond doubting to certainty.
        Purify our hearts,
            that the wrong desires may not only be kept under control,
            but may be completely taken away.

Strengthen our wills,
    that we may pass beyond resolving to doing,
    and beyond intention to action.

By your Holy Spirit,
    Break for us the habits we cannot break;
    Conquer for us the fears we cannot conquer;
    Calm for us the worries we cannot still;
    Soothe for us the sorrows no human comfort can ease;
    Answer for us the questions no human wisdom can answer.

O God, our Father, this day we rest our weakness in your strength, and our insufficiency in your completeness. Take us, and do for us what we cannot do, and make us what we cannot be; through Jesus Christ our Lord. Amen.

The Twentieth Sunday after Trinity

*O almighty and most merciful God, of thy bountiful good-
ness keep us, we beseech thee, from all things that may
hurt us; that we, being ready both in body and soul, may
cheerfully accomplish those things that thou wouldest have
done; through Jesus Christ our Lord.* Amen.

Epistle: Ephesians 5.15-21   *Gospel:* Matthew 22.1-14

O God, our Father, protect us from all that would hurt us
in body, mind, or spirit.

Protect us from all that would injure our bodies.
> From habits which would injure our health;
> From the greed or the self-indulgence which would
> leave us soft and flabby;
> From any practice that would make our body a less
> efficient servant of our mind:
>> Protect us, O God.

Protect us from all would injure our minds.
> From the mental laziness that will not think;
> From that preoccupation with cheap and trivial things
> which saps the ability of the mind to deal with the
> things which really matter;
> From the prejudice which blinds us to the truth and
> which makes us misjudge other people:
>> Protect us, O God.

Protect us from all that would injure our hearts.
From the pride that separates us from you;
From the self-righteousness which separates us from our fellow men and women;
From the self-will that will listen to no other voice, human or divine, than the voice of its own desires;
Protect us, O God.

And so grant that by your protection being
strong in body;
vigorous in mind;
pure in spirit,

we may be enabled to do the work which you need us to do; through Jesus Christ our Lord. Amen.

The Twenty-first Sunday after Trinity

Grant, we beseech thee, merciful Lord to thy faithful people pardon and peace, that they may be cleansed from all their sins, and serve thee with a quiet mind; through Jesus Christ our Lord. Amen.

Epistle: Ephesians 6.10-20   *Gospel:* John 4.46b-54

O God, our Father, lover of human souls, grant us today your pardon and your peace.

> For the sins of our lips;
>> For words untrue and words unclean and words unkind;
>
> For the sins of our hands;
>> For all careless work, for all wrong deeds,
>>> for any action which hurt another,
>>>> or which it made it easier for him to go wrong;
>
> For the sins of our minds;
>> For blindness to the truth, for refusal to face the facts,
>>> for all dishonest thinking;
>
> For the sins of our hearts;
>> For all pride, all wrong desires,
>>> and all false loves:
>>>> Forgive us, O God.

Grant us this day, O God,
> Peace within ourselves,
>> that our inner tensions may be taken away;

that we may no longer be torn in indecision;
that we may no longer be for ever halting between two opinions.

Grant us this day, O God,
Peace with our fellow men and women,
that we may not disturb the fellowship by disputing;
that we may never quarrel within our homes or outside them;
that we may live in unity with all.

Grant us this day, O God,
Peace with you,
that the certainty that you love us
may take all fear away;
that we may know,
that your love has forgiven us;
that your grace upholds us;
that your welcome awaits us.

And so grant that we may live at peace with ourselves, in fellowship with our fellow men and women, and at one with you; through Jesus Christ our Lord. Amen.

The Twenty-second Sunday after Trinity

Lord, we beseech thee to keep thy household the Church in continual godliness; that through thy protection it may be free from all adversities, and devoutly given to serve thee in good works, to the glory of thy Name; through Jesus Christ our Lord. Amen.

Epistle: Philippians 1.3-11   *Gospel:* Matthew 18.21-35

O God, our Father, bless your Church.

Help us always to remember that the Church is your family;

And so help us within the Church never to do anything to grieve your fatherly heart,

And never to do anything to turn to bitterness the brotherly love, which ought to be the very air and atmosphere of your Church.

Give your Church grace to live in all godliness.

In this generation give your Church grace to be,
adventurous in thought and resolute in action;
courageous in witness and generous in service.

In this generation give your Church grace to have,
wisdom in its mind, certainty in its message;
love in its fellowship and a passionate desire to win those who are still outside.

Keep your Church free from persecution from outside and from dissension inside.

Strengthen your Church within the world that it may stand
       Like a steadfast rock
         amid the shifting sands
           of doubt and unbelief;
       Like a clear light of goodness
         amid the falling of standards,
           and the lowering of ideals;
       Like a warm fire of love
         amid the coldness of selfishness
           and the callousness of self-seeking.

So help your Church,
       To accept nothing but your guidance;
       To serve nothing but your will;
       To seek nothing but your glory;

through Jesus Christ our Lord. Amen.

The Twenty-third Sunday after Trinity

O God, our refuge and strength, who art the author of all godliness: Be ready we beseech thee, to hear the devout prayers of thy Church; and grant that those things which we ask faithfully we may obtain effectually; through Jesus Christ our Lord. Amen.

Epistle: Philippians 3.17-21   *Gospel:* Matthew 22.15-22

O God, you are our refuge.

> When we are exhausted by life's efforts;
> When we are bewildered by life's problems;
> When we are wounded by life's sorrows:
>> We come for refuge to you.

O God, you are our strength.

> When our tasks are beyond our powers;
> When our temptations are too strong for us;
> When duty calls for more than we have to give to it:
>> We come for strength to you.

O God, it is from you that all goodness comes.

> It is from you that our ideals come;
> It is from you that there comes to us
>> the spur of high desire and the restraint of conscience.
> It is from you that there has come the strength
>> to resist any temptation,
>> and to do any good thing.

And now as we pray to you,

    Help us to believe in your love,
      so that we may be certain
      that you will hear our prayer;

    Help us to believe in your power,
      so that we may be certain
      that you are able to do for us
      above all that we ask or think;

    Help us to believe in your wisdom,
      so that we may be certain
      that you will answer,
      not as our ignorance asks,
      but as your perfect wisdom knows best.

All this we ask through Jesus Christ our Lord. Amen.

The Twenty-fourth Sunday after Trinity

O Lord, we beseech thee, absolve thy people from their offences; that through thy bountiful goodness we may all be delivered from the bands of those sins, which by our frailty we have committed: Grant this, O heavenly Father, for Jesus Christ's sake, our blessed Lord and Saviour. Amen.

Epistle: Colossians 1.3-12   *Gospel:* Matthew 9.18-26

O God, our Father, you know us better than we know ourselves, and you know our weakness and our frailty.

Our minds are too easily led.
　Too often we are too easily influenced
　　by specious arguments,
　　which seek to prove what we would like to be true.
Our hearts are too easily swayed.
　Too often we are fickle and inconstant in our devotion,
　　and so the fascination of the false love
　　lures us from the true.
Our memories are too forgetful.
　We forget what we have learned;
　We forget the experiences,
　　which should have been a lasting warning to us;
　We forget the gratitude we ought ever to remember.
Our wills are too weak.
　We can resolve, but we cannot do;
　We can know, but we cannot obey;
　We can decide, but we cannot carry out.

So by our continual sinning we have become the slaves of sin.

> There are things we do, not because we want to do them, but because we cannot help doing them.
>
> There are habits which we long to break, and cannot break.
>
> There are things we do, because, although we know they are wrong, we cannot stop ourselves.

O God, forgive us for all past sin. Break by your power the chains that bind us; and in the future so let your recreating power remake us that for us also the old things may pass away and all things may become new; through Jesus Christ our Lord. Amen.

The Twenty-fifth Sunday after Trinity

Stir up, we beseech thee, O Lord, the wills of thy faithful people; that they, plenteously bringing forth the fruit of good works, may of thee be plenteously rewarded; through Jesus Christ our Lord. Amen.

Lesson: Jeremiah 23.5-8   *Gospel:* John 6.5-14

O God, our Father, strengthen our wills this day.

> Clear sight, that we may recognize the things that matter and the things that do not matter;
>
> A sense of proportion, that we may see which things are worth getting excited about, and which things are not important;
>
> Wisdom, that in all life's choices we may be enabled to choose aright:
>
>> Grant us these things, O God.
>
> Independence, that popularity or unpopularity may not affect our decisions;
>
> Perseverance, that, having begun a good thing, we may not lay it down until we have completed it;
>
> Determination, that nothing may deflect us from our chosen way:
>
>> Grant us these things, O God.

O God, our Father, by your grace make us fruitful in all good works.

> Kindness, that no one in need may ever appeal to us in vain;

138

Generosity, that we may be concerned, not with how little, but with how much we can give;

Loyalty, that, though all deny you, we may still be true;

Love, that like our Master we may be among our fellow men and women as those who serve:
> Grant us these things, O God.

O God, our Father, grant us at the end to enter into our reward.

Help us to live so close to our blessed Lord
> That death may be only an entering into his nearer presence;
>
> That we may so live that even here and now we may know the life which is eternal;
>
> That we may so live each day that at the end of all days we may hear you say, Well done!

Hear these our prayers; through Jesus Christ our Lord. Amen.

II

Holy Days

Saint Andrew's Day

Almighty God, who didst give such grace unto thy Holy Apostle Saint Andrew, that he readily obeyed the calling of thy Son Jesus Christ, and followed him without delay: Grant unto us all, that we, being called by thy holy Word, may forthwith give up ourselves obediently to fulfil thy holy commandments; through the same Jesus Christ our Lord. Amen.

Epistle: Romans 10.9-21   *Gospel:* Matthew 4.18-22

O Lord Jesus, help us to accept your call as Andrew did.

Help us, as Andrew did, to hear your call above the many voices of the world.

Grant that

> the claims of business;
> the attractions of pleasure;
> the cares of this world

may not make us fail to hear your call.

Help us, as Andrew did, to obey at once; and grant that we may not put off until tomorrow that decision which we ought to make today.

Help us, as Andrew did, to give ourselves wholly to your obedience.

Cleanse us from

> the self-will, which would make us want nothing but our own way;
> the lack of discipline, which would make us refuse to make the effort which obedience demands;

the subjection to the fear, or the desire for the favour, of others, which would make us refuse your commandments;

the love of comfort and security, which would make us take the easy rather than the right way.

Help us here and now to accept your call, that one day we may share your glory. This we ask for your love's sake. Amen.

Saint Andrew's Day is 30th November.

Saint Thomas the Apostle

*Almighty and everlasting God, who for the more confirma-
tion of the faith didst suffer thy holy Apostle Thomas to be
doubtful in thy Son's resurrection: Grant us so perfectly
and without all doubt, to believe in thy Son Jesus Christ,
that our faith in thy sight may never be reproved. Hear us,
O Lord, through the same Jesus Christ, to whom with thee
and the Holy Ghost, be all honour and glory, now and for
evermore.* Amen.

Epistle: Ephesians 2.19-22   *Gospel:* John 20.24-31

O God, our Father, it encourages us to know that even an
Apostle lost and found his faith.

There is so much in this life to take our faith away:
    The problems to which there is no solution;
    The questions to which there is no answer;
    The sorrows for which there is no comfort;
    The tears of things for which there is no consolation;
    The pains for which there is no cure;
    The tragedies for which there is no explanation.

    Sometimes even the door of prayer seems shut;
    Sometimes the burden of life and the mystery of death
        overwhelm us;
    Sometimes we feel that there is no fidelity in humankind
        and no answer from you.

    Sometimes we feel battered and buffeted by the storm
        of life;

Sometimes our minds are bewildered and our hearts are broken.

At times like that help us to remember Thomas who lost and found his faith again.

Help us to remember our blessed Lord who on his Cross cried out: 'My God, my God, why have you forsaken me?' And help us like him to hold on until the dark changes to the dawn again, and we can say in perfect faith, made stronger by the testing, 'Father, into your hands I commend my spirit.'

Hear this our prayer; through Jesus Christ our Lord. Amen.

Saint Thomas's Day is 21st December.

The Conversion of Saint Paul

O God, who, through the preaching of the blessed Apostle Saint Paul, hast caused the light of the Gospel to shine throughout the world: Grant, we beseech thee, that we, having his wonderful conversion in remembrance, may show forth our thankfulness unto thee for the same, by following the holy doctrine which he taught; through Jesus Christ our Lord. Amen.

Lesson: Acts 9.1-22   *Gospel:* Matthew 19.27-30

O God, today we thank you for Paul, the apostle to the Gentiles, the apostle to us.

> We thank you for the grace which changed him
> > from the persecutor to the servant of the faith;
> Help us also so to love you and so to surrender to you,
> > that we too may find the grace
> > > which makes all things new.

> We thank you for his skill and wisdom
> > in argument and in debate, in preaching and in writing,
> > > through which many in many lands were brought to Jesus Christ;
> Help us to take every talent and every gift which we possess,
> > and to lay them on the altar of your service,
> > > that we too may be used to bring others to you.

We thank you for the courage and the endurance
   with which he travelled over land and sea
      to preach the gospel;
Help us to be ready to give, and even to sacrifice,
   our time, our energy, our money,
      to help and serve your Church wherever we live.

We thank you for the way in which he faced
   slander and persecution, imprisonment, trial and
   death.
Help us also, if need be,
   to suffer rather than to be false to the faith.

We thank you for the gospel
   which he preached;
Help us also so to live
   that by the wisdom of our words and the power of
   our example,
      others may be moved to give their hearts to you.

This we ask through Jesus Christ our Lord. Amen.

The date of the Conversion of Saint Paul is 25th January.

The Presentation of Christ in the Temple, commonly called, The Purification of Saint Mary the Virgin

Almighty and everliving God, we humbly beseech thy Majesty, that, as thy only-begotten Son was this day presented in the temple in substance of our flesh, so we may be presented unto thee with pure and clean hearts, by the same thy Son Jesus Christ our Lord. Amen.

Lesson: Malachi 3.1-5   *Gospel:* Luke 2.22-40

O God, we remember how this day our blessed Lord was presented as a little baby in the Temple in Jerusalem. Grant that even so we may present ourselves as an offering to you.

Help us to offer our bodies to you,
   that we may live in purity and in chastity
      all the days of our life.

Help us to offer our minds to you,
   that all our thoughts may be pure and clean,
   that we may ever seek the truth,
      and never be satisfied with any false thing;
   that we may think with that utter honesty,
      which never evades the facts.

Help us to offer our hands to you,
   that you may enable us to use them
      in usefulness,
         to earn a living for ourselves and for those we love;
      in kindness,
         to help those who are in need of help;
      in gentleness,
         to soothe and to heal another's sorrow and pain.

148

Help us to offer our voices to you,
   that you may use us as heralds of your grace,
   and that through us comfort and courage
     may be brought to those who need them.
Help us to give our hearts to you,
   that we may so love you,
   that we may seek nothing but to please you,
   and fear nothing but to grieve you.

So help us to give back to you the life we owe, offering ourselves to you, body, soul and spirit, that in your service we may find our freedom and our peace and our life; through Jesus Christ our Lord. Amen.

The date of the Purification is 2nd February.

Saint Matthias's Day

O Almighty God, who into the place of the traitor Judas didst choose thy faithful servant Matthias to be of the number of the twelve Apostles: Grant that thy Church, being always preserved from false Apostles, may be ordered and guided by faithful and true pastors; through Jesus Christ our Lord. Amen.

Lesson: Acts 1.15-26 *Gospel:* Matthew 11.25-30

O God, you are the fountain of all truth; we ask you to protect your Church from all false teaching.

Protect the Church
From all teaching and preaching which would destroy people's faith;
From all that removes the old foundations
without putting anything in their place;
Form all that confuses the simple,
that perplexes the seeker,
that bewilders the wayfarer.

And yet at the same time protect the Church
From the failure to face new truth;
From devotion to words and ideas
which the passing of the years has rendered unintelligible;
From all intellectual cowardice
and from all mental lethargy and sloth.

O God, send to your Church teachers,
  Whose minds are wise with wisdom;
  Whose hearts are warm with love;
  Whose lips are eloquent with truth.

Send to your Church teachers
  Whose desire is to build and not to destroy;
  Who are adventurous with the wise,
    and yet gentle with the simple;
  Who strenuously exercise the intellect,
    and who yet remember that the heart has reasons
    of its own.

Give to your Church preachers and teachers who can make
known the Lord Christ to others because they know him
themselves; and give to your Church hearers, who, being
freed from prejudice, will follow truth as blind men long for
light. This we ask through Jesus Christ our Lord. Amen.

Saint Matthias's Day is 24th February.

The Annunciation of the Blessed Virgin Mary

We beseech thee, O Lord, pour thy grace into our hearts; that, as we have known the incarnation of thy Son Jesus Christ by the message of an angel, so by his cross and passion we may be brought unto the glory of his resurrection; through the same Jesus Christ our Lord. Amen.

Lesson: Isaiah 7.10-15   *Gospel:* Luke 1.26-38

O God, Father of your Son our Saviour Jesus Christ, help us to know Jesus

>   in his incarnation;
>   in his cross and death;
>   in his resurrection and his risen power.

Help us to know him in his incarnation.

>   Help us to remember,
>   That he grew up, as we must grow up;
>   That he learned in obedience, as we have to learn;
>   That he worked for a living, as we have to work;
>   That he was tempted, as we are tempted;
>   That he knew
>   the failure of love,
>   the malice of enemies,
>   the faithfulness of friends;
>   That he was
>   the helper of all in need,
>   the healer of the sick,
>   the feeder of the hungry,

the comforter of the sad,
the friend of those who had no friends,
and whom all men despised.

Help us to know him in his death.

Help us to remember,
That he loved us and gave himself for us;
That he was obedient unto death;
That he gave his life a ransom for many,
a ransom for us.

Help us to know him in his resurrection and in his risen power.

Help us to remember,
That he conquered death,
and that he is alive for evermore;
That he is with us always,
to the end of time and beyond.

So help us to know our Lord in the beauty of his life, in the wonder of his death and in the power of his resurrection. This we ask for your love's sake. Amen.

The date of the Annunciation is 25th March.

Saint Mark's Day

O Almighty God, who hast instructed thy holy Church with the heavenly doctrine of thy Evangelist Saint Mark: Give us grace, that, being not like children carried away with every blast of vain doctrine, we may be established in the truth of thy holy Gospel; through Jesus Christ our Lord. Amen.

Epistle: Ephesians 4.7-16   *Gospel:* John 15.1-11

O God, we thank you for all those in whose words and in whose writings your truth has come to us.

> For the historians, the psalmists and the prophets,
> who wrote the Old Testament;
> For those who wrote the Gospels and the Letters
> of the New Testament;
> For all who in every generation
> have taught and explained and expounded and preached
> the word of Scripture:
> We thank you, O God.

Grant, O God, that no false teaching may ever have any power to deceive us or to seduce us from the truth.

> Grant, O God, that we may never listen to any teaching
> which would encourage us to think
> sin less serious, vice more attractive,
> or virtue less important;

Grant, O God, that we may never listen to any teaching
which would dethrone Jesus Christ from the topmost
place;
Grant, O God, that we may never listen to any teaching
which for its own purposes perverts the truth.

O God, our Father, establish us immovably in the truth.

Give us minds which can see at once
the difference between the true and the false;
Make us able to test everything,
and to hold fast to that which is good;
Give us such a love of truth,
that no false thing may ever be able to lure us
from it.

So grant that all our lives we may know, and love, and live
the truth; through Jesus Christ our Lord. Amen.

Saint Mark's Day is 25th April.

Saint Philip and Saint James's Day

O Almighty God, whom truly to know is everlasting life: Grant us perfectly to know thy Son Jesus Christ to be the way, the truth, and the life; that, following the steps of thy holy Apostles, Saint Philip and Saint James, we may stedfastly walk in the way that leadeth to eternal life; through the same thy Son Jesus Christ our Lord. Amen.

Epistle: James 1.1-12   *Gospel:* John 14.1-13

O God, our Father, we remember that Jesus said: I am the way, the truth, and the life.

Help us to find in Jesus
>The way that leads from earth to heaven;
>The way that leads from time to eternity;
>The way that leads from the things that are visible
>>to the things that are invisible;
>
>The way that leads to you.

Help us to find in Jesus
>The truth about ourselves,
>>so that we may see both what we are
>>and what we were meant to be;
>
>The truth about life that we may know
>>that the way to gain life
>>is to spend life,
>>that the cross
>>is the way to the crown;
>
>The truth about you,
>>so that we may know that in Jesus
>>we see exactly what you are like.

Help us to find in Jesus
    The life that is real life;
    The life that even on earth is a foretaste of heaven;
    The life that is your life;
    The life that not even death can extinguish.

And grant that we may ever walk the way your great apostles walked, so that with them we may enter into life eternal; through Jesus Christ our Lord. Amen.

    St Philip and St James's Day is 1st May.

Saint Barnabas the Apostle

O Lord God Almighty, who didst endue thy Holy Apostle Barnabas with singular gifts of the Holy Ghost: Leave us not, we beseech thee, destitute of thy manifold gifts, nor yet of grace to use them alway to thy honour and glory; through Jesus Christ our Lord. Amen.

Lesson: Acts 11.22-30   *Gospel:* John 15.12-16

Let us think of the life of Barnabas and let us pray
that our lives may become like his.

Let us think of Barnabas as the son of consolation (Acts 4.36).

Help us, O God, like Barnabas ever to be a comfort to the sad, a friend to the lonely and a consolation to the broken-hearted.

Let us think of Barnabas giving up his possessions (Acts 4.37).

Help us, O God, like Barnabas to take all that we have and to use it in your service and in the service of our fellow men and women, and help us to remember that giving is always better than getting.

Let us think of Barnabas standing guarantor for Paul (Acts 9.27).

O God, our Father, help us like Barnabas to stand by anyone who is trying to live a new life; and help us never to condemn anyone because of the past, but always to help everyone who is making a new beginning.

Let us think of Barnabas sent to preach to the Gentiles (Acts 13.1).

O God, our Father, help us like Barnabas ever to desire to tell the story of Jesus to those who have not heard it; and, if we cannot ourselves go to other lands, make us to help the work by the offering of our prayers and the giving of our money; and make us to remember that there are many in our own country and in our own circle who have still to be brought to you.

Let us think of Barnabas with Paul in Lystra (Acts 14.12-20).

Help us, O God like Barnabas to witness for you even if it is difficult or dangerous to do so. So help us never to be ashamed of the gospel of Christ.

Give us, as you gave to Barnabas, the gifts we need to serve you in our time, and give us grace to use them; through Jesus Christ our Lord. Amen.

Saint Barnabas's Day is 11th June.

Saint John Baptist's Day

Almighty God, by whose providence thy servant John Baptist was wonderfully born, and sent to prepare the way of thy Son our Saviour, by preaching of repentance: Make us so to follow his doctrine and holy life, that we may truly repent according to his preaching; and after his example constantly speak the truth, boldly rebuke vice, and patiently suffer for the truth's sake; through Jesus Christ our Lord. Amen.

Lesson: Isaiah 40.1-11   *Gospel:* Luke 1.57-80

O God, our Father, help us in everything to follow the example of your servant John the Baptist.

Help us sincerely to repent.

> Show us the ugliness and the evil of our lives;
> Show us the harm we have done,
>   and the heartbreak that we have caused;
> Show us how we have shamed ourselves, disappointed those who love us, and grieved you.
> Make us truly sorry for all our sins and our mistakes, and help us to show our sorrow by living better in the days to come.

Help us like John constantly to speak the truth.

> Keep us from twisting the truth to conceal our own faults;
> Keep us from evading the truth we do not wish to see;

Keep us from silencing the truth, because we are more afraid to offend others than we are to disobey you;
Save us from speaking or from acting a lie,
and save us from false words and from cowardly silence.

Help us like John boldly to rebuke vice.
Keep us from being censorious or arrogant, self-righteous or fault-finding;
But help us never to be silent
in the presence of injustice or impurity;
Grant that we may never see another drifting or rushing to disaster without speaking the word of warning we ought to speak in love.

Help us like John patiently to suffer for the truth.
Grant that we may set allegiance to the truth above all worldly success;
Grant that we may be ready to face loneliness and unpopularity for the sake of the truth;
Grant that we may follow the truth wherever it leads, that we may obey the truth whatever it demands, that we may speak the truth whatever it costs.

So grant that living the truth we may be the true servants of you who are the God of truth; through Jesus Christ our Lord. Amen.

Saint John Baptist's Day is 24th June.

161

Saint Peter's Day

O Almighty God, who by thy Son Jesus Christ, didst give to thy Apostle Saint Peter many excellent gifts, and commandest him earnestly to feed thy flock: Make, we beseech thee, all Bishops and Pastors diligently to preach thy holy Word, and the people obediently to follow the same, that they may receive the crown of everlasting glory; through Jesus Christ our Lord. Amen.

Lesson: Acts 12.1-11   *Gospel:* Matthew 16.13-19

O God, our Father, through Jesus Christ you called Peter to care for the flock of your Church. Bless all those who are pastors and preachers and leaders for your people.

Help them to be,
> Diligent in their study and their preparation;
> Earnest in their prayer and their devotion;
> Faithful and loving in their visitation;
> Sincere and honest in their preaching.

Help them to be,
> Wise in administration;
> Loving and forgiving in their dealings with others, especially with those who are difficult;
> Honest in their thinking so that other thinkers may respect them;
> Clear in their speaking so that simple folk may hear them gladly.

162

Bless all the members of your Church.
Grant that,

> They may come to Church with expectation;
> They may worship in truth and sincerity;
> They may listen with humility.
> Give them minds which are eager to learn,
> and memories that are retentive to remember,
> And grant that they may go out into the world
> > To practise what they have heard,
> > And to live what they have learned.

And so grant that pastors and people may be united in love for each other, in service of all, and in witness for you; through Jesus Christ our Lord. Amen.

Saint Peter's Day is 29th June.

Saint James the Apostle

Grant, O merciful God, that as thine holy Apostle Saint James, leaving his father and all that he had, without delay was obedient unto the calling of thy Son Jesus Christ, and followed him; so we, forsaking all worldly and carnal affections, may be evermore ready to follow thy holy commandments; through Jesus Christ our Lord. Amen.

Lesson: Acts 11.27-12.3   *Gospel:* Matthew 20.20-28

Let us remember how James with John left everything to follow Jesus (Mark 1.19, 20).

O Lord, Jesus Christ, help us as James did to set loyalty to you above all earthly things. Grant that no matter what the cost we may do what you order and go where you send.

> Help us to set any task to which you call us above any earthly career. Help us to remember that money and worldly success can cost too much, and help us to set obedience to you above the claims of any earthly person or thing; and grant that our love of you may surpass even the dearest and the closest human tie.

Let us remember how James with John was with Jesus at the raising of Jairus' daughter, on the Mount, in the Garden (Mark 5.37; 9.2; 14.33).

O Lord Jesus, make us such that we will be fit to be your closest friends. Make us such that we may ever see your vision and share your work, and enter into your ordeal. Make us such that you will be able to use us as voices to speak for you and hands to serve you.

Let us remember how James with John asked for the highest place (Mark 10.35-45).

O Lord Jesus, help us with James and John never to doubt that you will come into your kingdom and that you will one day give your own reward to those who are your faithful servants, but help us like them also to learn that true greatness lies in service, and that he who would be first must be the servant of all.

Let us remember how James died a martyr for his Lord (Acts 12.2).

O Lord Jesus, give us the loyalty which will make us ready to do and to endure all things for you. Make us faithful all our days, down even to the gates of death, that in the end we may receive the crown of life.

All this we ask for your love's sake. Amen.

Saint James the Apostle's Day is 25th July.

165

Saint Bartholomew the Apostle

O Almighty and everlasting God, who didst give to thine Apostle Bartholomew grace truly to believe and to preach thy Word: Grant, we beseech thee, unto thy Church, to love that Word which he believed, and both to preach and receive the same; through Jesus Christ our Lord. Amen.

Lesson: Acts 5. 12-16   *Gospel:* Luke 22. 24-30

O God, our Father, you have always been speaking to men and to nations, and you are still speaking to us.

Give us grace to listen to your word.

> Grant that we may not be so busy with the world's affairs that we have no time to listen to your voice. Grant that the voice of our own desires may not be speaking so insistently that we become deaf to your word.

Give us grace to receive your word.

> Grant that we may never reject your word because it speaks to us the truth which we do not want to hear. Grant that we may never shut our ears to your word because it calls us to a way which we do not want to take.

Give us grace to believe your word.

> Grant to us to believe that your commands are meant for us and that your promises are true for us. Grant to us to believe that you will never make a demand from us which you will not help us to perform, and that you will never make a promise that you will not fulfil.

166

Give us grace to love your word.

Grant that we may ever turn to your word to find light for our minds, guidance for our footsteps, and comfort for our hearts.

Give us grace to preach your word.

Grant that we may be eager to share with others that which we have learned from you, and that we may be able to lead others to love you because we love you ourselves.

Give us grace to live your word.

Grant that what we hear with our ears, we may understand with our minds, and receive into our hearts, and live out in our lives.

This we ask through Jesus Christ our Lord. Amen.

Saint Bartholomew's Day is 24th August.

Saint Matthew the Apostle

O Almighty God, who by thy blessed Son didst call Matthew from the receipt of custom to be an Apostle and Evangelist: Grant us grace to forsake all covetous desires, and inordinate love of riches, and to follow the same thy Son Jesus Christ, who liveth and reigneth with thee and the Holy Ghost, one God, world without end. Amen.

Epistle: II Corinthians 4.1-6   *Gospel:* Matthew 9.9-13

O God, our Father, we know that we cannot forget the world because we have to live in it. We know that we dare not disregard the world, because it is your world, and the work of the world has to go on. We cannot entirely neglect money and material things because we have to earn a living for ourselves and for those whom we love. But at the same time help us to see things in their proper proportion and to keep things in their proper place.

> Grant that we may never be so immersed in the things of time that we forget the things of eternity.
>
> Grant that we may never set material profit and gain above the claims of honesty and honour.
>
> Grant that we may never be so concerned with getting that we forget about giving.
>
> Grant that we may never be so concentrated upon our own concerns that we forget the appeal of those in need.

Deliver us from all covetousness, and from the desire to possess what we have not got. Give us grace always to make the best of what we have, and give us the gift of contentment with our lot.

Give us in our lives the right and the true ambition, the ambition to find our greatness in serving others, and the ambition to put into life more than we take out.

So save us from all selfishness, and put into our lives the spirit of him who, though he was rich, yet for our sakes became poor, and who loved us and gave himself for us.
This we ask for your love's sake. Amen.

Saint Matthew's Day is 21st September.

Saint Michael and All Angels

O Everlasting God, who hast ordained and constituted the services of Angels and men in a wonderful order: Mercifully grant, that as thy holy Angels alway do thee service in heaven, so by thy appointment they may succour and defend us on earth; through Jesus Christ our Lord. Amen.

Lesson: Revelation 12.7-12   *Gospel:* Matthew 18.1-10

O God, our Father, we know that your angels go willingly and obediently on any task to which you send them. In your mercy send them to us

For the enlightenment of our minds in knowledge;
For the guidance of our footsteps in wisdom;
For our help in every time of difficulty and danger;
For our defence in every hour of temptation.

Grant that they may be to us

The messengers,
  who tell us of your will;
The guides,
  who show us where we ought to go;
The helpers,
  who aid us
    when we are upon an engagement very difficult;
The protectors,
  who defend us against the assaults of the Evil One.

170

Make us even upon earth to feel around us and about us the powers of heaven, so that we may know that there is always with us a power which is not our power, to help us to overcome evil and to do the right, and so to live victoriously; through Jesus Christ our Lord. Amen.

The day of Saint Michael and All Angels is 29th September.

Saint Luke the Evangelist

Almighty God, who calledst Luke the Physician, whose praise is in the Gospel, to be an Evangelist, and Physician of the soul: May it please thee, that, by the wholesome medicines of the doctrine delivered by him, all the diseases of our souls may be healed; through the merits of thy Son Jesus Christ our Lord. Amen.

Epistle: II Timothy 4.5-15   *Gospel:* Luke 10.1-7a

O God, our Father, we remember today that you called Luke the beloved doctor to be the writer of a Gospel and a missionary of the Kingdom. Give to us this day healing of body, mind and spirit.

Give us health of body.

> Make us fit to do our work and to earn a living for ourselves and for those we love. Rid us of such habits and self-indulgences as would injure our bodies, and which would make us less fit to serve you and to serve our fellow men and women. Help us to remember that our bodies are meant to be the temple and the dwelling-place of your Holy Spirit, and that it is our duty to offer them as a living sacrifice to you.

Give us health of mind.

> Keep our thoughts from dwelling on evil, soiled or forbidden things. Give us honesty, sincerity, and openness of mind, that we may recognize, understand and obey the truth. Give us peace of mind that we may be saved

172

from the tension and from the strain, from the worry and from the anxiety, which make life collapse and break down. Give us a healthy mind in a healthy body.

Give us health of spirit.

Protect us from the temptations which would injure our purity and defend us from the sins which are always ready to fascinate and to seduce us. So cleanse us that we may be pure in heart and so see you; and so help us to wait on you that our strength may be daily renewed.

So grant that, healed and purified, strengthened and renewed, in body, mind and spirit, we may serve you and serve our fellow men in gladness, in peace, and in power; through Jesus Christ our Lord. Amen.

Saint Luke the Evangelist's Day is 18*th October.*

Saint Simon and Saint Jude, Apostles

*O Almighty God, who hast built thy Church upon the
foundation of the Apostles and Prophets, Jesus Christ himself being the head corner-stone: Grant us so to be joined
together in unity of spirit by their doctrine, that we may be
made an holy temple acceptable unto thee; through Jesus
Christ our Lord.* Amen.

Epistle: Jude 1-8   *Gospel:* John 15.17-27

O God, our Father, we thank you for those on whom your
Church is founded and built:

    For the apostles,
      who lived and who died,
        to bring the gospel to a world which had never
        known it;
    For the prophets,
      who fearlessly proclaimed your truth,
      and who without fear and without favour
        spoke to others what you had spoken to them.

Above all we thank you for Jesus Christ, the foundation
and the head corner-stone, on whom the Church is built
and by whom the Church is sustained.

Grant unto us in our day and generation that true unity of
spirit which will make us one.

Help us at all times,
> To hold one faith;
> To serve one Lord;
> To live in one love;
> To seek one goal.

To that end us keep us
> From the disharmony which divides;
> From the disunity which disturbs the peace;
> From the disputing which separates those who should
> be one.

Grant that
> We may never love systems
>> more than we love Jesus Christ;
> We may never love doctrines
>> more than we love our fellow men and women;
> We may never make creeds
>> a barrier to divide rather than a bond to unite.

So grant that built on one common foundation, holding one common faith, loving one common Lord, your Church may be a fit dwelling for your Holy Spirit; through Jesus Christ our Lord. Amen.

St Simon and St Jude's Day is 28*th October.*

All Saints' Day

O Almighty God, who hast knit together thine elect in one communion and fellowship, in the mystical body of thy Son Christ our Lord: Grant us grace so to follow thy blessed Saints in all virtues and godly living, that we may come to those unspeakable joys, which thou hast prepared for them that unfeignedly love thee; through Jesus Christ our Lord. Amen.

Lesson: Revelation 7.2-12   *Gospel:* Matthew 5.1-12

Eternal God, make us this day to remember the unseen cloud of witnesses who compass us about:

> Those who in every age and generation
>> witnessed to their faith in life and in death;
>
> Those who by their courage and their sacrifice
>> won for us the freedom and the liberty we enjoy;
>
> Those who served their fellow men
>> at the cost of pain, of persecution and of death;
>
> Those for whom all the trumpets sounded
>> as they passed over to the other side;
>
> Those whom we have loved and who have gone to be with you,
>> and whose names are written on our hearts.

Help us to walk worthily of those in whose unseen presence life is lived. Help us to have in our lives

> Their courage in danger;
> Their stedfastness in trial;
> Their perseverance in difficulty;

Their loyalty when loyalty is costly;
Their love which nothing can change;
Their joy which nothing can take away.

So grant to us in your good time to share with them the blessedness of your nearer presence, that we also may come to that life,

Where all the questions are answered;
Where all the tears are wiped away;
Where we shall meet again, never to be separated from
    them, those whom we have loved and lost awhile;
Where we shall be for ever with our Lord.

So grant to us in this life never to forget those who have gone before, so that in the life to come we may share their blessedness; through Jesus Christ our Lord. Amen.

All Saints' Day is 1st November.

III

Prayers for All Seasons

ALL OF LIFE

A Prayer of William Bright for the right spirit in worship

Almighty God, from whom every good prayer cometh, and who pourest out on all who desire it the spirit of grace and supplication: deliver us, when we draw nigh to thee, from coldness of heart and wanderings of mind, that with steadfast thoughts and kindled affections we may worship thee in spirit and in truth: through Jesus Christ our Lord. Amen.

The Reading Lesson: Luke 18.9-14

Prayer

O God, our Father, our life reaches out in ever-widening circles; bless us in each one of them.

Bless us in our homes and help us to remember all that we owe to them.

Bless us in our school and help us to learn well and to play fair.

Bless us in our university and college and help us to use to the full every opportunity which is given to us to equip our minds with knowledge and to widen our horizons.

Bless us in the place where we work and help us to be workers who will never need to be ashamed of anything they do or make.

Bless us in our town and help us to put as much and more into the life of the community as we take out.

Bless us in our church; make us in our church to worship with reverence and with gladness to serve the church with whatever gifts we have.

Bless us in our country, and help us to study, to learn and to train that we may be good citizens of it.

Bless us in the world, and in our day bind the nations together in peace.

A Prayer from the Coptic Liturgy of St Cyril

O God of love, who hast given us a new commandment through thine only-begotten Son, that we should love one another, even as thou didst love us the unworthy and the wandering, and gavest thy beloved Son for our life and salvation: we pray thee give us, thy servants, in all time of our life on earth, a mind forgetful of past ill-will, a pure conscience, sincere thoughts and a heart to love our brethren: for the sake of Jesus Christ, thy Son, our Lord and Saviour. Amen.

The Blessing

The grace of the Lord Jesus Christ be with us all.   Amen.

JESUS' NAMES FOR HIS PEOPLE

The Opening Prayer

O God, our Father, give us at all times,
>Minds which are eager to seek;
>Memories which are strong to remember;
>Wills which are dedicated to obey;
>Hearts which are surrendered to love;
>Lives which are committed to service:

through Jesus Christ our Lord.   Amen.

The Reading Lesson: Luke 6.12-16

Prayer

Let us think of the names by which Jesus called his people.

He called them disciples, which means learners.

>Lord Jesus, help us day by day to learn more of this world's knowledge and more of your love, so that day by day we may become better equipped to be the servants of our fellow men and women, and so that day by day we may be more firmly bound to you.

He called them witnesses.

>Lord Jesus, help us never to be ashamed to show to all people that we belong to you, and grant that our lives may shine like lights in this dark world to lead others to you.

He called them apostles, which means ambassadors.

>Lord Jesus, help us to remember that you are sending us out to live and to speak for you and help us so to live that we shall always bring credit on the name we bear, and so that others may find in us the way to you.

He called them his friends.

Lord Jesus, you loved us so much that you died for us. Help us to be loyal and true to you as friends should be and never at any time to let you down.

A Prayer of Queen Anne

Almighty and Eternal God, the Disposer of all the affairs in the world, there is not one circumstance so great as not to be subject to thy power, nor so small but it comes within thy care; thy goodness and wisdom show themselves through all thy works, and thy loving kindness and mercy appear in the several dispensations of thy Providence. May we readily submit ourselves to thy pleasure and sincerely resign our wills to thine, with all patience, meekness and humility: through Jesus Christ our Lord.   Amen.

The Blessing

May God the Father bless us. May Christ the Son take care of us. The Holy Spirit enlighten us all the days of our life.

The Lord be our defender and keeper of body and soul now and for ever and to the ages of ages.   Amen.

RESPECT AND REVERENCE

The Opening Prayer

Help us, O God, to find here tonight,
  Wisdom to know what is right,
  And strength to do what is right.
 Enlighten our minds with your truth;
 Warm our hearts with your love;
 Fill our lives with your power,
  That we may go out to live for you: through Jesus
  Christ our Lord.   Amen.

The Reading Lesson: 1 Corinthians 12.12-27

Prayer

Give us, O God, at all times respect for ourselves,
  So that we may never do work of which we would be
  ashamed;
  So that we may never stoop to that which is mean and
  low;
  So that we may never do in the present that which in
  the future we would have cause to regret.

Give us, O God, at all times love for others,
  So that we may never refuse an appeal for help;
  So that we may help even before we are asked for help;
  So that we may never do anything which would injure or
  hurt anyone else in body or in mind;
  So that we may find our joy in service and not in selfish-
  ness; in giving and not in getting; in sharing and not in
  keeping.

Give us, O God, at all times reverence for you,
So that we may remember that wherever we are and whatever we do you see us;
So that we may always obey your commands;
So that we may fear nothing except to grieve you, and seek nothing except to please you.

A Prayer of Ludwig von Beethoven

We must praise thy goodness, that thou hast left nothing undone to draw us to thyself. But one thing we ask of thee, our God, not to cease thy work in our improvement. Let us tend towards thee, no matter by what means, and be fruitful in good works, for the sake of Jesus Christ our Lord. Amen.

The Blessing

May grace, mercy and peace, from God the Father, Son, and Holy Spirit, be with us all now and evermore. Amen.

FOR THOSE IN TROUBLE

A Prayer from John Calvin before listening to God's Word

O Lord, Heavenly Father, in whom is the fulness of light and of wisdom, enlighten our minds by the Holy Spirit, and give us grace to receive thy Word with reverence and humility, without which no one can understand thy truth. For Christ's sake, Amen.

The Reading Lesson: Psalm 95.1-7

Prayer

in need

O God, our Father, bless those for whom life is very difficult.

Those who have difficult decisions to make, and who honestly do not know what is the right thing to do;

Those who have difficult tasks to do and to face, and who fear that they may fail in them;

Those who have difficult temptations to face, and who know only too well that they may fall to them, if they try to meet them alone;

Those who have a difficult temperament and nature to master, and who know that they can be their own worst enemies;

Those who have difficult people to work with, those who have to suffer unjust treatment, unfair criticism, unappreciated work.

Those who are sad because some one they loved has died;

Those who are disappointed in something for which they hoped very much;

Those who have been hurt by the malice of their enemies, or, what is far more bitter, by the faithlessness and the disloyalty of their friends.

186

Bless us all tonight, O God, with whatever need we come to you.

A Prayer of Dean Henry Alford

O Lord, give us more charity, more self-denial, more likeness to thee. Teach us to sacrifice our comforts to others, and our likings for the sake of doing good. Make us kindly in thought, gentle in word, generous in deed. Teach us that it is better to give than to receive; better to forget ourselves than to put ourselves forward; better to minister than to be ministered unto. And unto thee, the God of Love, be all the glory and praise, both now and for evermore. Amen.

The Blessing

The grace of the Lord Jesus Christ, the love of God, and the fellowship of the Holy Spirit be with us all. Amen.

OURSELVES AND OTHERS

The Opening Prayer

O God, our Father, we have come to you now that you may make us able,

> To walk in your light;
> To act in your strength;
> To think in your wisdom;
> To speak in your truth;
> To live in your love;

so that when all the days are done we may come to dwell in your glory: through Jesus Christ our Lord. Amen.

The Reading Lesson: Matthew 7.1-12

Prayer

O God, our Father, you have told us that we must not judge others, if we ourselves do not want to be judged. Help us never to be too critical of each other.

Keep us from harshly criticizing the work of others, and help us to remember that we have no right to criticize anyone's work, unless we are prepared to do the job better, or at least give a hand with it.

Keep us from unsympathetically criticizing the pleasures of others. Help us to remember that different people have different ways of enjoying themselves, that different people like different kinds of music and games and books, and different ways of spending their leisure. Help us not to despise everything which we don't like.

Keep us from contemptuously or arrogantly criticizing the beliefs of others. Help us to remember that there are as many ways to the stars as there are those to climb them;

and help us never to laugh at anyone's belief, if that is the way he or she gets to God.

Help us always,

> To praise rather than to criticize;
> To sympathize rather than to condemn;
> To encourage rather than to discourage;
> To build up rather than to destroy;
> To think of people at their best rather than
>   at their worst.

A Prayer from the Fifth Century Liturgy of Malabar

Grant, O God, that the ears which have heard the voice of thy songs may be closed to the voice of clamour and dispute; that the eyes which have seen thy great love may also behold thy blessed hope; that the tongues which have sung thy praise may speak the truth; that the feet which have walked thy courts may walk in the region of light; that the bodies which have partaken of thy living Body may be restored to newness of life. Glory be to thee for thine unspeakable gift. Amen.

The Blessing

The grace of the Lord Jesus Christ be with us all. Amen.

THE GIFT AND THE TASK

The Opening Prayer

O God, you have said that you are specially near to those
who are childlike in heart. Give us
> A child's trust, that we may never doubt your love;
> A child's wonder, that we may be lost in wonder at the
>   beauty and the bounty of the universe and at the
>   miracle of your love for us;
> A child's love, that we may love you as a child ought
>   to love a father:

through Jesus Christ our Lord.   Amen.

The Reading Lesson: Matthew 18.1-6

Prayer

Help us, O God, at all times to do the things we ought to do.
To that end give us,
> Clear sight,
>> that we may know what to do;
> Courage,
>> to embark upon it;
> Skill,
>> to find a way through all its problems;
> Perseverance,
>> to bring it to its appointed end;
> Strength,
>> to resist all the temptations which would seek to
>> lure us aside.

So help us to begin, to continue and to end all things in you.

A Prayer of Dean Colet

O most merciful Father, who dost put away the sins of those who truly repent, we come before thy throne in the name of Jesus Christ, that for his sake alone, thou wilt have compassion upon us, and let not our sins be a cloud between thee and us. Amen.

The Blessing

The peace of God which passeth all understanding keep our hearts and minds in the knowledge and love of God, and of his Son Jesus Christ our Lord, and the blessing of God Almighty, the Father, the Son and the Holy Spirit, be amongst us and remain with us always. Amen.

FOR THOSE WE REMEMBER

The Opening Prayer

Teach us this night, O God,
>   how to master ourselves,
>   that we may serve others.

And help us this night so to see you, that through all the days of the week we may never forget you: through Jesus Christ our Lord.   Amen.

The Reading Lesson: Isaiah 1.12-18

Prayer

O God, our Father,

> Bless our friends and our loved ones and keep them safe from harm and danger.
>
> Bless our enemies and those who dislike us, and help us by caring for them to make them our friends.
>
> Bless those who are in pain of body, anxiety of mind, and sorrow of heart.
>
> Bless those who are lonely because death has taken a dear one from them.
>
> Bless those who are old and who now are left alone.
>
> Bless those who have made a mess of life and who know well that they have no one but themselves to blame.
>
> Bless those who have fallen to temptation and who are sorry now, and give them grace to begin again and this time not to fall.
>
> Bless all who are in trouble and help them to win their way through it.

Bless each one of us as you know we need.

A Prayer of John Tillotson

Give us, O Lord, a mind after thine own heart, that we may delight to do thy will, O our God; and let thy law be written on our hearts. Give us courage and resolution to do our duty, and a heart to be spent in thy service, and in doing all the good that possibly we can the few remaining days of our pilgrimage here on earth. Grant this, we humbly beseech thee, for the sake of Jesus Christ thy Son our Lord.   Amen.

The Blessing

And now may the blessing of the Lord rest and remain upon all his people in every land and of every tongue. The Lord meet in mercy all that seek him. The Lord comfort all that suffer and mourn. The Lord hasten his coming, and now give us and all his people peace.   Amen.

A THANKSGIVING FOR PEOPLE

The Opening Prayer

O God, our Father, we come to you tonight to find,
> Strength,
>> To keep our hearts pure;
>> To keep our minds clean;
>> To keep our words true;
>> To keep our deeds kind:

through Jesus Christ our Lord.   Amen.

The Reading Lesson: Psalm 119.9-16

Prayer

Tonight, O God, we bring our thanks to you, and specially our thanks for people.

> For those who are an example to us, and those who in their lives show us what life ought to be;
> For those who are an inspiration to us, and who fill us with the desire to make of life a noble thing;
> For those who are a comfort to us when life has hurt us;
> For those who are a strength to us, and in whose company we feel fit to tackle any task;
> For those who, although we do not know them personally, have by their words or by their writings influenced us for good;
> For those whose love and care and service and understanding we so often take for granted;
> For those who give us loyal friendship and for those who give us true love:
>> We this night thank you, O God.

And most of all we thank you for Jesus to be the Pattern of our lives, the Companion of our way, and the Saviour of our souls.

A Prayer of Richard Baxter

O thou Spirit of Life, breathe upon thy graces in us, take us by the hand and lift us up from earth, that we may see what glory thou hast prepared for them that love thee: through Jesus Christ our Lord. Amen.

The Blessing

Unto God's gracious mercy and protection we commit ourselves. The Lord bless and keep us. The Lord make his face to shine upon us and be gracious unto us. The Lord lift up the light of his countenance upon us, and give us peace, both now and evermore. Amen.

FOR ALL WRONG THINGS

The Opening Prayer

A Prayer of B. F. Westcott before reading the Bible

Blessed Lord, by whose providence all holy Scriptures were
written and preserved for our instruction, give us grace to
study them this and every day, with patience and love.
Strengthen our souls with the fulness of their divine teaching. Keep from us all pride and irreverence. Guide us in
the deep things of thy heavenly wisdom, and of thy great
mercy lead us by thy word unto everlasting life: through
Jesus Christ our Lord and Saviour. Amen.

The Reading Lesson: Luke 4.16-22

Prayer

O God, our Father, we have come to you tonight to say that
we are sorry for all the wrong things that we have done.

> For the work that we did carelessly;
> For the work that we have left half-finished;
> For the work that we have not even begun:
> > Forgive us, O God.

> For the people we have hurt;
> For the people we have disappointed;
> For the people we have failed when they needed us most:
> > Forgive us, O God.

> For the friends to whom we have been disloyal;
> For the loved ones to whom we have been untrue;
> For the promises we have broken;
> For the vows we have forgotten:
> > Forgive us, O God.

For the way in which we have disobeyed you;
For the way in which we have grieved you;
For our failure to love you as you have loved us:
    Forgive us, O God.

A Prayer of Polycarp

May God the Father, and the eternal High Priest, Jesus
Christ, build us up in faith and truth and love, and grant to
us our portion among the saints with all those who believe
on our Lord Jesus Christ. We pray for all saints, for kings
and rulers, for the enemies of the Cross of Christ, and for
ourselves we pray that our fruit may abound and we may be
made perfect in Christ Jesus our Lord. Amen.

The Blessing

May grace, mercy, and peace, from Father, Son, and Holy
Spirit, one God, rest upon us all now and abide with each
one of us henceforth and for evermore. Amen.

THOSE TO WHOM WE MATTER

The Opening Prayer

Lord Jesus, we know that you have rest for the tired.

Lord Jesus, we know that you have guidance for the perplexed.

Lord Jesus, we know that you have strength for the tempted.

Give us tonight your rest, your guidance, and your strength.
This we ask for your love's sake. Amen.

The Reading Lesson: Matthew 11.25-30

Prayer

O God, our Father, help us to remember that you know all about us.

Keep our thoughts so clean and pure that they may be fit for you to see.

Help us so to live that even our secret actions, the things we do when there is no man to see, may be fit to be open to your sight.

O God, our Father, we know that there are those who love us.

Help us never to do anything to hurt or disappoint them.

Help us never to do anything which would make us less fit to be loved.

O God, our Father, we know that there are those on whom we have an influence.

Help us never to do anything which would make it easier for them to go wrong.

Help us never to place temptation in their way.

Help us to remember that there are things in this world which cost too much, and that there are pleasures which can be too dearly bought. And help us to live so that life may be ever stronger and purer and kinder day by day, so that at the end of the days there may be nothing of which to be ashamed and nothing to regret.

A Prayer of Muhammad

O Lord, grant us to love thee; grant that we may love those that love thee; grant that we may do the deeds that win thy love. Make the love of thee to be dearer to us than ourselves, our families, than wealth, and even than cool water. Amen.

The Blessing

The love of God, the grace of our Lord Jesus Christ, the fellowship of the Holy Spirit be with us all, now and always. Amen.

RIGHT RELATIONSHIPS

The Opening Prayer

We have come to you, O God,
>To thank you for your past gifts to us;
>To receive strength for the present duties we must do;
>To find courage to face anything which the future may bring.

So let it be given unto us: through Jesus Christ our Lord. Amen.

The Reading Lesson: Proverbs 8.12-21

Prayer

O God, our Father, help us in our lives to have the right attitude to everyone.

Help us to have the right attitude to ourselves.
Keep us from
>The pride which makes us conceitedly pleased with ourselves;
>The false modesty which is an excuse for evading responsibility;
>The blindness which cannot see our own faults;
>The selfishness which puts self in the centre of everything.

Help us to have the right attitude to others.
Keep us from
>The critical spirit which looks for faults;
>The thoughtless spirit which never thinks of the feelings of others;
>The cowardice which is afraid of what others will say;

The desire to curry favour which makes us too intent
on pleasing others, even at the expense of honour, of
honesty and of truth.

Help us to have the right attitude to you.
Keep us from
The forgetfulness which never thinks of you;
The rebelliousness which takes its own way of things;
The irreverence which forgets that you are here.
Help us to think of ourselves, to think of others, and to
think of you as we ought.

A Prayer of J. H. Jowett

O God, our Father, we would thank thee for all the bright
things of life. Help us to see them, and to count them, and
to remember them, that our lives may flow in ceaseless
praise: for the sake of Jesus Christ our Lord. Amen.

The Blessing

The love of God, the grace of the Lord Jesus Christ, the
fellowship of the Holy Spirit be with us all, now and evermore. Amen.

TO GET RID OF AND TO GET

The Opening Prayer

O God, our Father, silence everything in us this night which
would keep us from hearing what you have to say to us.
Control our minds, that all our thoughts may be concentrated on you. And help us to find here light to shine upon
our path and strength to walk in it: through Jesus Christ
our Lord. Amen.

The Reading Lesson: Matthew 25.1-13

Prayer

O God, our Father, save us from everything which would
make life useless and ugly.

Save us from,

    The unteachable spirit which will not learn;

    The ungrateful spirit which never says thanks;

    The unhappy spirit which is filled with complaints and
      discontent.

Save us from,

    The disobliging spirit which grudges any help it has to
      give;

    The discourteous spirit which never thinks of the feel-
      ings of anyone else;

    The disobedient spirit which will take nothing but its
      own way.

Give us,

    A sense of responsibility,

      that we may know that we can neither live nor die
      to ourselves:

A sense of duty,
　　that we may leave nothing that we ought to do un-
　　done;
A sense of gratitude,
　　that we may offer thanks to you by trying to live
　　more nearly as you would have us to do.

A Prayer of Peter Marshall

O God, our Father, let us not be content to wait and see what will happen, but give us the determination to make the right things happen.

While time is running out, save us from the patience which is akin to cowardice.

Give us the courage to be either hot or cold, to stand for something, lest we fall for anything. In Jesus' Name. Amen.

The Blessing

The blessing of God, Father, Son and Holy Spirit, be upon us all now and stay with each one of us always. Amen.

The Opening Prayer

Give us this night, O Father,

    Reverence,

        to realize your presence;

    Humility,

        to know our own need;

    Trust,

        to ask your help;

    Obedience,

        to accept whatever you say to us:

so that it may this night be good for us to be here: through Jesus Christ our Lord. Amen.

The Reading Lesson: Matthew 16.24-27

Prayer

Help us, O God, to remember that all great things have their price.

Help us to remember that,

    There is no achievement without work;

    There is no learning without study;

    There is no skill of body or of mind without discipline.

Help us to remember that,

    There is no purity without vigilance;

    There is no friendship without loyalty;

    There is no love without the death of self.

Help us to remember that,

    There is no joy without service;

    There is no discipleship without devotion;

    There is no crown without a cross.

So help us to be willing to pay the price that we may enter into our reward.

An Intercession from the Liturgy of St Mark

We most earnestly beseech thee, O thou lover of mankind, to bless all thy people, the flocks of thy fold. Send down into our hearts the peace of heaven, and grant us also the peace of this life. Give life to the souls of all of us, and let no deadly sin prevail against us, or any of thy people. Deliver all who are in trouble, for thou art our God, who settest the captives free; who givest hope to the hopeless and help to the helpless; who liftest up the fallen; and who art the haven of the shipwrecked. Give thy pity, pardon and refreshment to every Christian soul, whether in affliction or error. Preserve us in our pilgrimage through this life from hurt and danger, and grant that we may end our lives as Christians, well-pleasing to thee and free from sin, and that we may have our portion and lot with all thy saints: for the sake of Jesus Christ, our Lord and Saviour. Amen.

The Blessing

The grace of the Lord Jesus Christ be with us all. Amen.

LIFE'S NECESSITIES

The Opening Prayer

O God, our Father, tonight we come to you to listen and to learn.

Take from us

> The laziness which will not learn,
> The prejudice which cannot learn,

and give us

> Minds adventurous to think,
> Memories strong to remember,
> Wills resolute to do.

This we ask for Jesus' sake.   Amen.

A Collect from the Book of Common Prayer for use before reading Scripture

Blessed Lord, who hast caused all holy Scriptures to be written for our learning; Grant that we may in such wise hear them, read, mark and inwardly digest them, that by patience, and comfort of thy holy Word, we may embrace and ever hold fast the blessed hope of everlasting life which thou hast given us in our Saviour Jesus Christ.   Amen.

The Reading Lesson: Romans 8.31-39

Prayer

O God, Lord of all good life, give us the things which will enable us to make something worthwhile out of life.

> Discipline to accept the necessity of study and of work;
> A sense of proportion to see the things which really matter;

The ability to take the long view that we may never sell the most precious things for a moment's cheap pleasure:
> Grant us these things, O God.

Perseverance that we may never leave a task uncompleted;
Concentration that we too may say, This one thing I do;
Patience that we may never give up and never give in:
> Grant us these things, O God.

The teachable spirit which realizes its own ignorance;
The humble spirit which will accept advice and which will not resent rebuke;
The diligent spirit that whatever our hand finds to do we may do with our might:
> Grant us these things, O God.

So help us to bear the yoke in our youth that in the days to come we may serve you and serve our fellow men and women well: through Jesus Christ our Lord.

The Blessing

The blessing of God, Father, Son and Holy Spirit be on us now and stay with us always. Amen.

FAITH, HOPE AND LOVE

The Opening Prayer

Give us this night, O God,

    Ears open to hear your word;

    Minds ready to accept your truth;

    Wills ready to accept your commands;

    And above all hearts ready to answer to your love:

through Jesus Christ our Lord. Amen.

The Reading Lesson: Luke 4.14-30

Prayer

So faith, hope, love abide, these three; but the greatest of these is love.

O God, our Father, grant us

  The faith which is sure and certain of what it believes;

  The faith which unhesitatingly believes in your promises
    and unquestioningly accepts your commands;

  The faith which is loyal to you in any situation.

  The hope which will never despair;

  The hope that no disappointment can quench;

  The hope which in spite of failure will never give in.

  The love which is always ready to forgive;

  The love which is always eager to help;

  The love which is always happier to give than to get.

And so grant that living in faith, in hope, in love, we may live like Jesus.

A Prayer of Thomas Arnold

O Lord, we have a busy world around us. Eye, ear, and thought will be needed for all our work to be done in the

world. Now ere we again enter into it, we would commit
eye, ear, and thought to thee. Do thou bless them and keep
their work thine, that as through thy natural laws our hearts
beat and our blood flows without any thought of ours for
them, so our spiritual life may hold on its course at those
times when our minds cannot consciously turn to commit
each particular thought to thy service: through Jesus Christ
our Lord. Amen.

The Blessing

The grace of the Lord Jesus Christ be with us all. Amen.

FOR OTHERS

The Opening Prayer

O God, our Father, help us tonight,

>To see ourselves in all our weakness,

>To see you in all your power.

Then help us to take our weakness to your power, that in your love you may give us strength to do the things we cannot do, and to be the things we cannot be: through Jesus Christ our Lord.   Amen.

The Reading Lesson: Galatians 6.1-10

Prayer

Tonight, O God, we want to forget ourselves and to remember others.

>Those who are ill and in pain;
>Those who are waiting for an operation;
>Those who are waiting for a doctor's diagnosis and verdict and who fear the worst:
>>Bless all such.

>Those who are nervous, worried, anxious, afraid of life;
>Those who are on the verge of a nervous breakdown;
>Those who feel that they cannot cope with life:
>>Bless all such.

>Those who are hungry and cold;
>Those who are refugees with no home;
>Those who are unemployed with no work;
>Those who are persecuted and those who have lost their freedom:
>>Bless all such.

Out of your great riches supply the need of those distressed in body, mind or heart.

A Prayer of Thomas à Kempis

Grant that in all things we may behave ourselves so as befits a creature to his Creator, a servant to his Lord. Make us diligent in all our duties, watchful against all temptations, pure and temperate and moderate in thy most lawful enjoyments, that they may never become a snare to us. Help us, O Lord, to act towards our neighbour that we may never transgress the royal law of thine, of loving him as ourselves. Finally, we beseech thee, O Lord, to sanctify us throughout, that our whole spirit, soul and body, may be preserved blameless unto the coming of the Lord Jesus Christ: to whom with thee and the Holy Spirit be all honour and glory for ever. Amen.

The Blessing

The grace of the Lord Jesus Christ, the love of God, the fellowship of the Holy Spirit be with us all this night and stay with us always. Amen.

THE NECESSARY KNOWLEDGE

The Opening Prayer

O God, our Father, the life of all who live, the strength of the weak, and the hope of all who are in distress, put this night your truth into our minds and your purity into our hearts. Strengthen our wills that we may be able always to choose the right and always to refuse the wrong. And help us at all times to bear one another's burdens and to forgive one another's faults that we may obey your law and become daily more like our blessed Lord. This we ask for your love's sake.   Amen.

The Reading Lesson: Ecclesiastes 7.1-12

Prayer

O God, our Father, give us the knowledge which will enable us to live life well.

Help us really to know ourselves. Help us to know
> Our own ignorance, that we may ever be teachable and willing to learn;
> Our own weakness, that we may be ever on our guard against the temptations which so easily overcome us, unless we are on the watch;
> Our own strength, that we may use to the full the gifts and talents which you have given to us.

Help us to know our fellow men and women. Help us to know
> That they are your children, so that we may ever respect and reverence all men as sons of God;
> That they are our brothers, so that, as members of one great family, we may ever be ready to help one another;

That there is so much bad in the best of us and so much
good in the worst of us that it ill becomes any of us to
find fault with the rest of us.

Help us really to know you. Help us to know
Your holiness, that we may know that fear which is the
beginning of wisdom;
Your purity, that we also being pure in heart may see you;
Your love, that we may love you as you have first loved
us.

A Prayer of Rabindranath Tagore

When the heart is hard and parched up, come upon me with
a shower of mercy.

When grace is lost from life, come with a burst of song.

When tumultuous work raises its din on all sides, shutting
me out from beyond, come to me, my Lord of silence,
with thy peace and rest.

When my beggarly heart sits crouched, shut up in a
corner, break open the door, my king, and come with the
ceremony of a king.

When desire blinds the mind with delusion and dust, O
thou holy One, thou wakeful, come with thy light and
with thy thunder.

The Blessing

The grace of the Lord Jesus Christ be with us all. Amen.

THE SEVEN VIRTUES

The Opening Prayer

Give us, O God,
>Wisdom to know;
>Humility to accept;
>Strength to do

your will for us, so that, having walked in faith, in obedience and in fidelity, we may one day hear you say: Well done! : through Jesus Christ our Lord.   Amen.

The Reading Lesson: Luke 12.35-48

Prayer

Let us pray to God to give us the Seven Virtues which we have always thought the greatest virtues of all.

O God, our Father, give us the virtues which will make life strong and lovely.

>Fidelity, that we may be for ever true to friendship, to love and to you;
>Hope, that not all earth's setbacks and disappointments may ever drive us to despair;
>Love, that we may feel towards our fellow men and women as you feel to them;
>Prudence, that we may be wise to choose, not that which is at the moment attractive, but that which is to our ultimate good;
>Justice, that we may never be swayed by passion or by prejudice, but that in honour and in honesty we may be fair to others;

Courage, that no cowardly and unworthy fear may ever keep us from doing the right thing and taking the right road;

Self-control, that we may be master of every impulse and of every passion, and so able to serve others because we can rule ourselves.

So let your divine grace make beautiful our human life.

A Prayer of King Alfred

Lord God Almighty, shaper and ruler of all creatures, we pray thee for thy great mercy to guide us to thy will, to make our minds steadfast, to strengthen us against temptation, to put far from us all unrighteousness. Shield us against our foes, seen and unseen; teach us in order that we may inwardly love thee before all things with a clean mind and a clean body. For thou art our Maker and Redeemer, our help and our comfort, our trust and our hope, now and ever. Amen.

The Ascription of Praise

To God the Father, who loved us, and made us accepted in the Beloved;

To God the Son, who loved us, and loosed us from our sins by his own blood;

To God the Holy Spirit, who sheddeth the love of God abroad in our hearts;

To the one true God be all love and all glory for time and for eternity. Amen.

FOR THOSE IN NEED

The Opening Prayer

Eternal and everblessed God, you have taught us to call you
Father, and you have surrounded us all our lives by your
fatherly love and care. Help us so to live that we may be
sons and daughters who bring joy and not sorrow to their
Father's heart: through Jesus Christ our Lord. Amen.

The Reading Lesson: Luke 7.1-10

Prayer

Tonight, O God, we pray to you for all those who are in
pain and distress of body or of mind.

Bless those who are ill; be specially near to those who
will never be well again; and ease the pain of those whose
pain is beyond human skill to help.

Bless those who are sad, those on whose dearest circle
the chill wind of death has blown, and comfort those
whom no one else can comfort.

Bless those who have had some great disappointment,

Those who have found a friend untrue;

Those who have found a lover faithless;

Those who have failed in something for which they
toiled;

Those to whom life has refused something on which they
set their hearts.

Bless those who are worried,

Those who are worried about their health;

Those who have an insoluble problem which must be
solved;

Those who have a difficult decision which must be taken;
Those who know that they must meet their testing time;
Those who are tempted and who fear that they may fall.

O God, our Father, we remember all this world's unfortunate ones,
Refugees without a home and without a state;
Those who are persecuted for their faith;
Those who are suffering for their loyalty to some principle which is dearer to them than comfort and than life.

Grant that all in trouble may remember your promise that when they pass through the waters you will be with them, and grant that they may find it true.

A Prayer of the Venerable Bede

Open our hearts, O Lord, and enlighten us by the grace of thy Holy Spirit, that we may seek what is well-pleasing to thy will; and so order our doings after thy commandments, that we may be found meet to enter into thine unending joys: through Jesus Christ our Lord. Amen.

The Blessing

Now may grace, mercy and peace from Father, Son and Holy Spirit, one God, rest upon us all and abide with each one of us henceforth and for evermore. Amen.

THE IMPORTANT AND THE
UNIMPORTANT

The Opening Prayer, A Prayer before the reading of Scripture

O Lord Jesus, who hast told us in thy holy Word that thou lovest us, and gavest thy life for us, keep us in that love, and help us more and more to read, love, and understand thy Word, that we may learn of thee, and of the Holy Spirit and of thy Father in heaven. Amen.

The Reading Lesson: Luke 12.22-31

Prayer

O God, our Father, forgive us that we so often give our best to the wrong things.

Sometimes we put far more enthusiasm and thought and effort into our pleasures and our games and our amusement than we do into our work.

Sometimes we keep our best behaviour for strangers and our worst behaviour for our own homes; and often we treat our nearest and dearest with a discourtesy and a disregard we would never show to strangers.

Sometimes we get irritated and annoyed and angry about things which in our calmer moments we know do not matter.

Sometimes we lose our temper in an argument about trifles.

Sometimes we allow very little things to cause a quarrel with a friend.

Help us to see what is important and what is unimportant, so that we may never forget the things that matter, and so that we may never allow the things which do not matter to matter too much.

A Prayer of St Augustine

> O Thou, from whom to be turned is to fall,
>> to whom to be turned is to rise,
>> and in whom to stand is to abide for ever;
> Grant us
>> in all our duties thy help;
>> in all our perplexities thy guidance;
>> in all our dangers thy protection;
>> and in all our sorrows thy peace:
>>> through Jesus Christ our Lord.   Amen.

The Blessing

Christ, our Saviour, come thou to dwell within us, that we may go forth with the light of thy hope in our eyes, and thy faith and love in our hearts.   Amen.

SPEAKING AND LISTENING

The Opening Prayer

Eternal God, whom to know is life eternal and whom to serve is fulness of joy, help us to know you with our minds, to love you with our hearts, to serve you with our lives, so that our lives may be garrisoned with your peace and radiant with your glory: through Jesus Christ our Lord. Amen.

The Reading Lesson: 1 Samuel 3.1-10

Prayer

O God, help us tonight to say to you, just as Samuel did: Speak, Lord, your servant is listening. Speak to us the word we need, and help us to hear it.

Speak to us
> The word of encouragement when we are discouraged and depressed;
> The word of warning when we are likely to go astray;
> The word of comfort when life has hurt us;
> The word of guidance when we do not know what to do and where to go;
> The word of strength to enable us to resist our temptations;
> The word of power to make us able for work and ready for any burden.

Whatever word we need, speak it to us now.

Take from us everything which would keep us from hearing your voice.

Take from us
> The inattentive mind and the wandering thoughts;
> The cold heart and the weak will;

The self-will which disregards the truth;

The prejudice which cannot hear or see the truth, but which sees only what it wants to see;

The desire not to be disturbed, which is afraid of the truth.

Help us in this place to hear your word, and to go out and obey it.

A Prayer of St Basil

O Lord our God, teach us, we beseech thee, to ask thee aright for the right blessings. Steer thou the vessel of our life towards thyself, thou tranquil haven of all storm-tossed souls. Show us the course wherein we should go. Renew a willing spirit within us. Let thy Spirit curb our wayward senses, and guide and enable us unto that which is our true good, to keep thy laws, and in all our works evermore to rejoice in thy glorious and gladdening presence. For thine is the glory and the praise from all thy saints for ever and ever. Amen.

The Blessing

The blessing of God, the Father, the Son and the Holy Spirit, be on us now and stay with us always. Amen.

DIFFICULT TO LIVE WITH

The Opening Prayer

Make us tonight, O God,
  sorry for our sins and grateful for your gifts;
Make us
  certain of your power and will to help.
So grant that tonight we may find forgiveness for the past,
and strength to do better in the future: through Jesus Christ
our Lord. Amen.

The Reading Lesson: Romans 15.1-6

Prayer

O God, forgive us for the faults which make us difficult to
live with.

> If we behave as if we were the only people for whom
>   life is difficult;
> If we behave as if we were far harder worked than
>   anyone else;
> If we behave as if we were the only people who were
>   ever disappointed, or the only people who ever got
>   a raw deal;
> If we are far too self-centred and far too full of self-
>   pity:
>   Forgive us, O God.

> If we are too impatient to finish the work we have
>   begun;
> If we are too impatient to listen to some one who wants
>   to talk to us, or to give some one a helping hand;
> If we think that other people are fools, and make no
>   attempt to conceal our contempt for them:
>   Forgive us, O God.

222

If we too often rub people the wrong way;
If we spoil a good case by trying to ram it down some-
one's throat;
If we do things that get on people's nerves, and go on
doing them, even when we are asked not to:
Forgive us, O God.

Help us to take the selfishness and the ugliness out of life
and to do better in the days to come.

A Prayer of St Augustine

Blessed are all thy saints, O God and King, who have
travelled over the tempestuous sea of this life, and have
made the harbour of peace and felicity. Watch over us who
are still in our dangerous voyage; and remember such as lie
exposed to the rough storms of trouble and temptations.

Frail is our vessel, and the ocean is wide; but, as in thy
mercy thou hast set our course, so steer the vessel of our
life toward the everlasting shore of peace, and bring us at
length to the quiet haven of our heart's desire, where thou,
O our God, art blessed, and livest and reignest for ever and
ever. Amen.

The Blessing

May the Lord lead us when we go, and keep us when we
sleep, and talk with us when we wake; and may the peace
of God which passeth all understanding, keep our hearts
and minds in Christ Jesus our Lord. Amen.

LIFE'S NEEDS

The Opening Prayer

O God, our Father, you are the Truth; give us your truth
tonight.

> Help us to see the truth about ourselves,
>> that we may see ourselves as we really are, and not
>> as we think we are.
>
> Help us to see the truth about life,
>> that we may see what we ought to do, and not only
>> what we want to do.
>
> Help us to see the truth about you,
>> that we may really know your wisdom and your
>> love,

so that we may trust you wholly and obey you fully:
through Jesus Christ our Lord.   Amen

The Reading Lesson: Matthew 26.6-13

Prayer

O God, our Father, give us your help whatever life is like.

> In difficulty keep us from discouragement,
>> and in failure from despair.
>
> In joy help us never to forget to sympathize with others
>> who are sad, and in sorrow help us to hope for the
>> future as well as to remember the past.
>
> In success keep us from conceit,
>> and when things go well keep us from thinking
>> that we do not need you.
>
> Help us to remember that there is no situation
>> in which you cannot help us,
>
> And no time in which we do not need your help.

O God, our Father, bless those for whom the evening is a difficult time;

> Those who are so lonely that they do not know what to do;
>
> Those who are so sad that they do not know how to go on;
>
> Those who are in such pain that they are afraid of the night;
>
> Those who are so worried that sleep is impossible;
>
> Those who are in such need that they do not know how the needs of tomorrow can be met.

Bless everyone in trouble of body or of mind as each one needs.

An Ancient Prayer

O God, Author of Eternal Light, do thou shed forth continual day upon those who watch for thee, that our lips may praise thee, our life may bless thee, our meditations may glorify thee: through Jesus Christ our Lord. Amen.

The Blessing

The grace of the Lord Jesus Christ go with us all. Amen.

THAT WE MAY DO WHAT
WE OUGHT TO DO

The Opening Prayer

Lord Jesus, who said, I am the Way,
    Show us tonight the way we ought to go,
Lord Jesus, who said, I am the Truth,
    Show us this night the truth we ought to know.
Lord Jesus, who said, I am the Life,
    Show us tonight what real life is.
This we ask for your love's sake.   Amen.

The Reading Lesson: Luke 1.46-55

Prayer

O God, our Father, grant that nothing may stop us doing
what we ought to do and being what we ought to be.

Grant that,
    Laziness may not stop us doing the work we ought to do;
    Fear may not keep us from taking the stand we ought to
        take;
    Selfishness may not stop us giving the service we ought
        to give.

Grant that,
    Ingratitude may not stop us being as grateful as we ought
        to be;
    Indifference may not stop us caring as we ought to care;
    Self-will may not stop us obeying you as we ought to
        obey.

Grant that,
    Lack of perseverance may not stop us finishing the things
        we have begun;

Lack of discipline may not make us take the easy way;
Lack of foresight may not make us choose the things
which bring nothing but regret.

Grant that,
Despair may not make us stop trying;
Discouragement may not make us give up and give in;
Pessimism may not take our hope away.

Grant us,
Such wisdom of mind;
Such strength of will;
Such devotion of heart,

that we may not even desire to do anything except the
things that please you: through Jesus Christ our Lord.
Amen.

A Prayer of Lancelot Andrewes

Take us, we pray thee, O Lord of our life, into thy keeping
this night and ever. O thou Light of lights, keep us from
inward darkness; grant us so to sleep in peace, that we may
arise to work according to thy will: through Jesus Christ
our Lord. Amen.

The Blessing

The blessing of God be on us now and stay with us always.
Amen.

FOR EACH ONE'S NEED

The Opening Prayer

O God, our Father, make us this evening so aware of your presence that,

> The thoughtless may be compelled to think;
>
> The ungrateful may be compelled to give thanks;
>
> Those about to do some wrong thing may be restrained;
>
> That the sad may be comforted; the depressed encouraged; the lonely cheered;
>
> And that those who are happy may be still happier:

through Jesus Christ our Lord. Amen.

The Reading Lesson: Matthew 11.25-30

Prayer

O God, our Father, there are no two of us here with the same need. You know our needs. Bless us as each one of us needs. Specially bless those who are in the middle of some specially difficult time:

> Those who have some specially difficult task to face or some specially difficult examination to sit;
>
> Those who have some specially difficult problem to solve;
>
> Those who have some specially difficult decision to take;
>
> Those who have some specially difficult temptation to resist;
>
> Those who have some specially baffling doubt through which to think their way.

Speak to those who are

> Evading some decision;
>
> Shirking some task;
>
> Putting off some duty;

> Playing with fire;
> Wasting their time;
> Throwing away their opportunities.

Tell them that they dare not bring shame to themselves and disappointment to those who love them.

Speak to those who are successful, that they may be kept from all pride and self-conceit; speak to those who are too self-confident, that they may not be riding for a fall; speak to those who are too sure that they are right and too sure that everyone else is wrong, that they may be kept from intolerance. Help those who are shy. Remember those who are in disgrace and in prison, and keep them from despair.

A Prayer for Consecration

Our Father, may Christ's spirit of duty and service ennoble all that we do. Inspire us with the faith, that, in ways beyond our knowing, our work is a blessing to others. From day to day may there be nothing in our work of which we shall be ashamed when the sun is set, nor in the eventide of life when our task is done: through Jesus Christ our Lord. Amen.

The Blessing

The blessing of God be on us all now, and stay with each one of us always. Amen.

LIFE'S OPPORTUNITIES

The Opening Prayer

Grant, O God, that these few minutes with you may send
us out again

> More kind to others;
> More honest with ourselves;
> More loyal to you:

through Jesus Christ our Lord.   Amen.

The Reading Lesson: Matthew 25.14-30

Prayer

O God, our Father, you have made life full of opportunities.
Help us to miss none of these opportunities when they come
to us.

Help us not to miss the opportunities of learning and help
us to work, to study, to train, and to accept discipline that
we may

> Deepen our lives;
> Enrich our minds;
> Learn our trade;
> Master our craft;
> Be efficient at our job;
> Be equipped for our profession.

Help us never to miss the opportunities of helping others
that we may be ready

> To share with the poor;
> To sympathize with the sad;
> To encourage the depressed;
> To help those who have made mistakes back on
> to the rails again;

> To lend a hand to those who are finding things difficult.

Help us never to miss an opportunity to show where we stand that we may

> Set a Christian example wherever we are;
> Always make it easier for others to do and be good, and never make it easier for them to do any wrong thing;
> Always be good advertisements for our faith and for our church.

So help us to grasp every opportunity you send, and to use every gift you have given us that we may make life what you meant it to be.

A Prayer for the Lord's Day

O Lord, God of our life, who hast given us the rest of this sacred day; grant that the benediction of its restfulness may abide upon us throughout the week. Enable us to carry the influence of its consecration into all we do; let the praises of our lips rendered to thee this day become praise in our lives. May the power of thy love be with us in every duty, that by pureness, by knowledge, and by tenderness we may glorify thee; through Jesus Christ our Lord.   Amen.

The Blessing

The grace of the Lord Jesus Christ be with us all.   Amen.

TRUE HUMILITY

The Opening Prayer

O God, our Father, for this short time of worship direct and
control our thoughts that we may think only of you.
Grant us
       Reverence as we remember your glory;
       Penitence as we remember your holiness;
       Gratitude as we remember your love.
So grant that we may rise from our worship
       With knowledge deepened;
       With love kindled;
       With strength to live more nearly as we ought:
through Jesus Christ our Lord.   Amen.

The Reading Lesson: II Corinthians 5.17-21

Prayer

O God, our Father, give to us the humility which

       Realizes its ignorance;
       Admits its mistakes;
       Recognizes its need;
       Welcomes advice;
       Accepts rebuke.

Save us from pride in our knowledge, and make us to think
   of the great ocean of truth all undiscovered before us.
Save us from pride in our achievement, and make us to
   remember all that we still have to do.
Save us from pride in our performance, and make us to remember how far short of perfection our best must still
   fall.

Help us in the days ahead,
> To study with diligence;
> To learn with eagerness.

And give us
> A retentive memory to remember that which we have learned;
> And a resolute will to put it into action.

A Prayer of Robert Louis Stevenson

Go with each of us to rest; if any awake, temper to them the dark hours of watching; and when the day returns, return to us, our sun and comforter, and call us up with morning faces and with morning hearts, eager to labour, eager to be happy, if happiness should be our portion, and if the day be marked for sorrow, strong to endure it. Amen.

The Blessing

The grace of the Lord Jesus Christ be with us all. Amen.

THE NECESSITIES OF FRIENDSHIP

The Opening Prayer

Grant unto us, in our hearts, O God, as we come to you,
        Gratitude for all your gifts;
        Sorrow for all our sins;
        Trust in your power and will to help.
So grant that we may find here tonight:
        Forgiveness for the past;
        Strength for the present;
        Confidence that the future can bring nothing that in
           your strength we cannot meet:
through Jesus Christ our Lord.   Amen.

The Reading Lesson: I Thessalonians 5.12-24

Prayer

Keep us, O God, from all the things which make friendship impossible.

Keep us from
        The sarcastic tongue;
        The critical eye;
        The ears which love malicious gossip;
        The mind which thinks the worst;
        The heart whose only love is self-love.

Give us the things which will enable friendship to flourish.
Give us
        The ability to bear one another's burdens and to for-
           give one another's faults;
        The sympathetic, the unselfish and the understand-
           ing heart;

The temper and the tongue which are always under
control;
The determination to treat others as we would have
them treat us;
The tolerance which can always see the point of view
of others.

Help us to live ever remembering that in you we live and
move and have our being, and that life is always in your
sight.

An Ancient Prayer from the Gelasian Sacramentary

O God, who knowest us to be set in the midst of so many
and great dangers, that by reason of the frailty of our nature
we cannot always stand upright, grant to us such strength
and protection as may support us in all dangers and carry
us through all temptations: through Jesus Christ our Lord.
Amen.

The Blessing

The grace of the Lord Jesus Christ, the love of God, and
the fellowship of the Holy Spirit be upon us all now and
stay with each one of us this night and always.   Amen.

THIS WORLD AND THIS LIFE

The Opening Prayer

O God, our Father, be with us at our time of worship to-night.

When we pray, help us to concentrate our thoughts on
you.

When we listen to the reading of the Bible, help us to understand it, and to understand what it means for us.

When we sing your praise, help us to sing because we
really love you.

So help us tonight to worship you in spirit and in truth:
through Jesus Christ our Lord. Amen.

The Reading Lesson: Psalm 119.103-112

Prayer

O God, our Father, we thank you that you have made all
things and made them well.

We thank you for the world in which we live.

For the light of the day and the dark of the night;

For the glory of the sunlight, for the silver splendour of
the moon, and for the star-scattered sky;

For the hills and the sea, for the busy city streets, for the
open road and the wind on our faces:

We thank you, O God.

We thank you for ourselves.

For hands to work, and eyes to see, and ears to hear;

For minds to think, and memories to remember, and
hearts to love:

We thank you, O God.

We thank you for all that makes life worthwhile.
> For a task to do, and for health of body, for accuracy of hand and eye;
>
> For skill of mind and brain to do it;
>
> For homes and for friends and for loved ones:
>> We thank you, O God.

We thank you that this life is not the end.
> That we are preparing ourselves for another and a greater life;
>
> That there is a place where all questions will be answered, and all hopes realized;
>
> That we will meet again those whom we have loved and lost awhile:
>> We thank you, O God.

We thank you most of all for Jesus, our Friend and our Example, our Saviour and our Lord.

Help us to try to deserve a little better all the gifts which you have given to us.

A Prayer of William Bright

O God, by whom the meek are guided in judgment, and light riseth up in darkness for the godly; grant us in our doubts and uncertainties the grace to ask what thou wouldst have us to do; that the Spirit of wisdom may save us from all false choices, and that in thy light we may see the light, and in thy straight path may not stumble: through Jesus Christ our Lord. Amen.

The Blessing

Lord, dismiss us with thy blessing, that we, inspired by this hour, may radiate light and life. Amen.

THE FRUIT OF THE SPIRIT

The Opening Prayer

O God, we come to you today for your help and your blessing.

> Lord, what we know not, teach us;
> Lord, what we have not, give us;
> Lord, what we are not, make us.

Hear this our prayer, through Jesus Christ our Lord. Amen.

(Prayers for Club and Hostel)

The Reading Lesson: Galatians 5.16-23

Prayer

Let us ask God to give us the fruit of his Spirit in our lives.

O God, our Father, give us the fruit of your Spirit in our lives.

Love, that we may love you as you have loved us, and that we may love others as you love them;

Joy, that we may be happy ourselves, and that we may help others to be happy;

Peace, that we may never again be restless, and worried, and nervous:

> Grant us these things, O God.

Patience, that we may no longer be irritable and in too big a hurry;

Kindness, that we may desire to give rather than to get, to share rather than to keep, to praise rather than to criticize, to forgive rather than to condemn;

Goodness, that we may be an example and a help to all:

> Grant us these things, O God.

Faithfulness, that through all the chances and the changes of life we may be true to ourselves, true to our loved ones, and true to you;

Gentleness, that we may be humble and not proud, and that we may never deliberately or carelessly hurt others;

Self-control, that no moment of impulse or of passion may make us to injure another or to bring shame on ourselves.

> Grant us these things, O God.

Help us so to live that on our lives there may be the reflection of the goodness of the Master, whose we are and whom we seek to serve.

A Prayer of Alfred the Great

Lord God Almighty, I charge thee of thy great mercy and by the token of thy holy rood (cross) that thou guide me to thy will and to my soul's need better than I can myself, that above all things I may inwardly love thee with a clean mind and a clean body; for thou art my Maker, my Help and my Hope: through Jesus Christ our Lord. Amen.

The Blessing

Now the God of peace, who brought again from the dead our Lord Jesus Christ, that great Shepherd of the sheep, make us perfect in every good work to do his will, working in us that which is well-pleasing in his sight, through Jesus Christ, to whom be glory for ever and ever. Amen.

COURTESY

The Opening Prayer

Help us, O God, to accept the disciplines which you are
wishing to lay upon us:

> The discipline of work and of study, that we may train
> and equip ourselves to do a good and useful day's
> work in the world;
>
> The discipline of prayer, that we may always live close
> to you;
>
> The discipline of service, that we may work for others
> and not for ourselves;
>
> The discipline of Christian living, that we may be true
> athletes and soldiers of our Master.

This we ask for your love's sake.   Amen.

The Reading Lesson: John 17.15-26

Prayer

Help us, O God, always to live in courtesy towards everyone whom we meet.

Help us

> Never to speak an angry, an impatient, a boorish, an
> impolite or a discourteous word;
>
> Never to make people feel a nuisance;
>
> Never to do things so grudgingly and so unwillingly
> that it is worse than not doing them at all;
>
> Never to give anything in such a way that the gift be-
> comes an insult;
>
> Never to treat people in such a way that it embarrasses
> them, or makes them feel small, or humiliates them.

Help us

> Always to be kind;
>
> Always to make people feel that they are welcome and that we care;
>
> Always to think of the feelings of others as much as we would wish them to think of ours;
>
> Always to respect and never to laugh at the things which are important and sacred to someone else.

Help us to walk looking unto Jesus, and to make him the pattern of our lives.

An Ancient Prayer of the Church

Bless all who worship thee from the rising of the sun to the going down of the same. Of thy goodness, give us; with thy love, inspire us; by thy Spirit, guide us; by thy power, protect us; in thy mercy, receive us, now and always. Amen.

The Blessing

Go forth into the world in peace; be of good courage; hold fast that which is good; render to no one evil for evil; strengthen the faint-hearted; support the weak; help the afflicted; honour all people; love and serve the Lord, rejoicing in the power of the Holy Spirit. And may the blessing of God Almighty, the Father, the Son and the Holy Spirit, be upon us and remain with us for ever. Amen.

EQUIPMENT FOR LIFE

The Opening Prayer

O God, our Father, make us so eager to seek the truth that
no study may be too difficult for us and no thinking too
adventurous.

Make us so willing to serve you and our world that no task
may be too wearisome for us and that no one may ever
appeal in vain to us for help and sympathy.

Make us so to feel your love for us that our hearts may go
out to you in wonder, love and praise.

This we ask for your love's sake. Amen.

The Reading Lesson: Colossians 3.23—4.5

Prayer

O God, we thank you for everything which widens our
knowledge and which equips us more fully for the task of
life and living.

For school and college and university;
For all wise teachers and instructors;
For those who teach not only by their words but also by
their example:
> We thank you, O God.

For all good books;
For all that makes available for us the wisdom which has
gone before;
For all the knowledge in the printed page with which we
can store our mind:
> We thank you, O God.

For all the precious things the past has left us;
For great poetry to linger in the memory;

For great pictures and sculpture to delight the eye;
For great music to sound in the ear and to thrill the
heart;
For all the heritage of beauty and loveliness into which
we have entered:
> We thank you, O God.

For radio and television; for computer and satellite;
For all that brings the distant places to our own fireside;
For every opportunity to gain knowledge and wisdom;
For everything whereby we learn our profession, our
trade, our craft;
And above all else for Jesus to show us how to use it all
for your sake and for the sake of mankind:
> We give you thanks, O God.

A Prayer of John Hunter

Grant, O Lord, that what we have said with our lips, we
may believe in our hearts and practise in our lives; and of
thy mercy keep us faithful to the end: for Christ's sake.
Amen.

The Blessing

May the blessing of God, Father, Son and Holy Spirit be
upon us all now and stay with each one of us always.
Amen.

THAT WE MAY BE USEFUL

The Opening Prayer

Eternal God, whom to know is life eternal,
> help us daily to know you better, that daily we may have life more abundantly.

Eternal God, whom to serve is perfect freedom,
> help us daily to do your will, that in doing your will we may find our peace.

Eternal God, whom to love is fulness of joy,
> help us daily to love you more, that daily we may come nearer to loving you as you first loved us.

This we ask for your love's sake. Amen.

The Reading Lesson: Luke 13.5-9

Prayer

Lord Jesus, who came not to be served but to serve, help us to live useful lives.

> Help us always to encourage, and never to discourage others; always to be readier to praise than to criticize, and to sympathize rather than to condemn.

> Help us always to help, and never to hinder others. Help us always to make the work of others easier and not harder. Help us not to find fault with the efforts of others, unless we are prepared to try to do the thing better ourselves. Make us more ready to co-operate than to object, and more ready to say yes than to say no when anyone appeals to us for help.

> Help us always to be a good example, and never a bad example. Help us always to make it easier for others to do the right thing, and never to make it easier for

them to go wrong. Help us to remember that what is safe for us may be dangerous for others. Help us always to take our stand beside anyone who is standing for the right.

So grant that indeed our lives may be like lights in the world.

A Prayer of St Augustine

Watch thou, dear Lord, with those who wake, or watch, or weep tonight, and give thine angels charge over those who sleep. Tend thy sick ones, O Lord Christ. Rest thy weary ones. Bless thy dying ones. Soothe thy suffering ones. Pity thine afflicted ones. Shield thy joyous ones. And all for thy love's sake.   Amen.

The Blessing

The grace of the Lord Jesus Christ be on us all and go with each one of us.   Amen.

THAT WE MAY BE TRUE

The Opening Prayer

Grant, O God, that we may never come to the end of any day without speaking to you and without listening to you speaking to us. And make us to feel you very near to us tonight as we end this day with you: through Jesus Christ our Lord. Amen.

The Reading Lesson: Romans 6.1-14

Prayer

O Lord Jesus, help us to be true to our faith and true to you, when things are difficult.

> When we have to stand alone;
> When loyalty to you makes us unpopular with our fellow men and women;
> When doing the right thing involves us in the dislike or in the laughter of others:
> > Help us still to be true.

Help us to be true to our faith and true to you, when it costs us something.

> When our Christian duty demands more of our time than we really want to give;
> When our Christian duty demands more of our money than we really want to give;
> When our Christian duty demands more of an effort than we really want to make:
> > Help us still to be true.

Help us to be true to our faith and true to you, when it is all against the things we instinctively want to do.

When we don't want to be unselfish;
When we have no desire to think of others;
When the last thing we want is to forgive someone who
has injured us;
>
> Help us still to be true.

Give us strength to do what we cannot do and to be what we cannot be; and help us to remember that by ourselves we can do nothing but that with you all things are possible.

A Prayer of Archbishop Laud

Grant, O God, that we may live in thy fear, die in thy favour, rest in thy peace, rise in thy power, reign in thy glory: for the sake of thy Son, Jesus Christ our Lord. Amen.

The Blessing

The peace of God sanctify us wholly, and may our whole spirit and soul and body be preserved blameless unto the coming of our Lord Jesus Christ. Amen.

RESCUE FROM OUR FAULTS

The Opening Prayer

Grant, O God, that, remembering your holiness, we may
come into your presence with penitence and godly fear.

Grant that, remembering your majesty, we may come into
your presence with reverence and with humility.

Grant that, remembering your love, we may come into your
presence with the trust and confidence of children who
know that they are coming to a Father who, no matter
what they have done, will not turn them away.   Amen.

The Reading Lesson: James 1.16-27

Prayer

O God, our Father, save us and rescue us from the faults to
which we are so prone.

Keep us,

> From saying one thing with our words and another
> with our deeds;

> From criticizing others for that which we allow in
> ourselves;

> From demanding standards from others which we our-
> selves make no effort to fulfil.

Keep us,

> From flirting with temptation and from playing with
> fire;

> From the indecision that cannot say yes or no and be
> done with it;

> From the reluctance to break with habits which we
> know are wrong.

Keep us,

> From trying to make the best of both worlds, and from trying to please both others and you;
>
> From living one way on Sunday and another on Monday;
>
> From anything which would keep us from giving our whole loyalty, our whole allegiance, our whole life, and whole heart to you.

A Great Prayer by an unknown Author

O Christ, our only Saviour, so dwell within us that we may go forth with the light of hope in our eyes, and the fire of inspiration on our lips, thy word on our tongue, and thy love in our hearts: through Jesus Christ our Lord. Amen.

The Blessing

May grace, mercy and peace from Father, Son and Holy Spirit, one God, be on us all now and stay with each one of us always. Amen.

THE GIFTS WE NEED

The Opening Prayer

O God, our Father, we have come to you tonight to find the strength and the beauty for life which we do not possess, and which can only come from you. Give us this night the gifts for which we pray: through Jesus Christ our Lord. Amen.

The Reading Lesson: Proverbs 2.1-15

Prayer

O God, give us the gifts which we need most of all.

Wisdom always to choose the right, and courage always to do it;
Strength to overcome temptation, and prudence ever to stay in the straight way;
Clear sight to see what to do, and perseverance never to give up trying to do it:
> Grant us these things, O God.

Diligence in study, and fidelity in work;
Purity in pleasure, and delight in simple things;
Honour in every action, and truth in every word:
> Grant us these things, O God.

Loyalty to our friends, and forgiveness to our enemies;
Sympathy for all in sorrow, help for all in need, understanding for those who have made mistakes;
Love for our fellow men and women, and love for you:
> Grant us these things, O God.

A Prayer from The Penitent Pilgrim *written in 1641*

Gracious Lord, in whom are laid up all the treasures of

knowledge and wisdom, direct us in the ways of life, remove from us the ways of death. Give us a soft and meek spirit, that we may help the succourless, and comfort the comfortless. O our Lord, pardon us for the neglect of this duty, and make us to redeem the time with a cheerful constancy. Amen.

The Blessing

The grace of the Lord Jesus Christ be with us all. Amen

FOR THOSE TO WHOM WE OWE SO MUCH

The Opening Prayer

Help us, O God, so to meet you today that we may go out knowing you better, loving you more, and to serve you more faithfully: through Jesus Christ our Lord. Amen.

The Reading Lesson: I John 4.7-12

Prayer

O God, our Father, we thank you for all the people you have given to us to whom we owe more than we can ever repay.

> For those who are an example to us, and who have shown us what life should be;
> For those who are an inspiration to us, and who fill us with the desire and the determination to do better;
> For those whose judgment we respect, and to whom we know that we can go for guidance and for advice;
> For those who, we know, will understand, even if we have to tell them of some foolish mistake that we have made or some bad thing that we have done;
> For those to whom we are not ashamed or afraid to go and ask for help:
>> We thank you, O God.

For those who help us,
> To bear our sorrows;
> To solve our problems;
> To conquer our temptations;
> To live more nearly as we ought;
> And above all else for Jesus Christ,

The pattern of our lives and the Saviour of our souls:
We thank you, O God.

An Ancient Prayer

Help us, O Lord, always to wait for thee, to wish for thee, and to watch for thee, that at thy coming again thou mayest find us ready: for thy sake we ask it. Amen.

The Blessing

The love of God, the grace of our Lord Jesus Christ, the fellowship of the Holy Spirit be with us all now and stay with each one of us always. Amen.

REMEMBERING OUR
RESPONSIBILITIES

The Opening Prayer

O God, our Father, speak to us today that here in your presence we may find knowledge of what you want us to do and strength to do it: through Jesus Christ our Lord. Amen.

The Reading Lesson: Galatians 5.16—6.2

Prayer

O God, Lord of all good life, give us in all things a true sense of responsibility.

Help us at all times to remember our responsibility to ourselves.

Help us,

> Never to act in such a way that we shall lose our self-respect;
>
> Never to let ourselves down by doing something which is mean and low, disloyal and dishonourable;
>
> Never to do anything which we would afterwards regret, perhaps spend the rest of our life regretting.

Help us at all times to remember our responsibility to our friends, and to those whom we love, and who love us.

Help us,

> Never to disappoint those who love us;
>
> Never to fail those who trust us;
>
> Never to bring grief or heartbreak to those in whose hearts we have a special place.

Help us at all times to remember our responsibility to others.

Help us,

> Not to be the kind of people who are always remembering their rights and always forgetting their duties;
>
> Not to be the kind of people who want to get everything out of life and to put nothing into it;
>
> Not to be the kind of people who do not care what happens to others so long as they are all right.

Help us at all times to remember our responsibility to you. Help us,

> To remember that we shall answer to you for the way we have used the gifts you gave us;
>
> To remember that we shall give account for all that we have been allotted in this life;
>
> To remember at all times how you have loved us and how Jesus died for us.

An Ancient Prayer

Thine is the day, O Lord, and thine is the night. Grant that the Sun of Righteousness may abide in our hearts to drive away the darkness of evil thoughts: through Jesus Christ our Lord. Amen.

The Blessing

The grace of the Lord Jesus Christ be with us all. Amen.

The Opening Prayer

Lord Jesus, you have promised to be there wherever your people come to meet with you. Help us to feel you very near tonight. Help us to hear your voice speaking to us when your word is read. And help us, when we pray, not only to speak to you, but also to listen to you speaking to us. This we ask for your love's sake.   Amen.

The Reading Lesson: Mark 10.35-45

Prayer

O God, our Creator and our Father, it is you who gave us life. Now teach us how to use life.

When we are thinking and planning what to do with life, help us to have the right kind of ambition.

Help us to think

Not of how much we can get out of life, but of how much we can put into life;

Not of how much we can get, but of how much we can give;

Not of the number of people we can use, but of the number of people to whom we can be of use.

Help us to think

Of money, not as something to spend on ourselves, but as something to share with others;

Of leisure time, not as something always to be used on pleasure, but as something which can be used to help the Church, this fellowship and the community in which we live;

Of work, not as a grim and stern necessity, but as that which makes life worthwhile, and help us to work, not for ourselves, and not for a master, but always for you and in the service of others.

Jesus was in the world as one who loved his fellow men and women and as one who served.

Help us always to be like him, that in his service we may find our perfect freedom and in doing his will our peace. This we ask for your love's sake. Amen.

St Francis' Prayer

Lord, make us instruments of thy peace.
   Where there is hatred, let us sow love;
      Where there is injury, pardon;
      Where there is discord, union;
      Where there is doubt, faith;
      Where there is despair, hope;
      Where there is darkness, light;
      Where there is sadness, joy;
         for thy mercy and thy truth's sake. Amen.

The Ascription and the Blessing

Now unto him that is able to keep us from falling, and to present us faultless before the presence of his glory with exceeding joy, to the only wise God, our Saviour, be glory and majesty, dominion and power, both now and ever. And may the blessing of God, Father, Son and Holy Spirit, be on us all now and stay with each one of us always. Amen.

THE LIFE WE LIVE

The Opening Prayer

O God, we have come to you tonight,
>> To thank you for all your gifts;
>> To ask your forgiveness for all our sins;
>> To receive your guidance for all our actions.

Hear us; forgive us; and direct us: for your love's sake.
Amen.

The Reading Lesson: Romans 12.9-21

Prayer

We thank you, O God, for all the interesting things in life.

> For music and for rhythm;
> For pictures and for plays;
> For radio and for television;
> For the things which make us laugh;
> For the things which command our interest;
> For the things which widen our knowledge:
>> We thank you, O God.

> For our work and for our study;
> And for the real satisfaction of a difficult task mastered, completed and done:
>> We thank you, O God.

O God, forgive us for the things in us which have spoiled life.
> If we have been lazy at work;
> If we have been difficult to get on with among friends, neighbours or colleagues;
> If we have been inconsiderate and ungrateful at home;
> If we have been forgetful of you:
>> Forgive us, O God.

O God, we thank you for all the possibilities of life. Help us,
  To work so hard;
  To study so diligently;
  To discipline ourselves so firmly,
that we may turn the possibilities into realities and so make
all our plans and dreams come true. So grant that we may
ever be,
  A credit to ourselves;
  A help to others;
  A joy to you.

Bless our friends and our neighbours and our loved ones.
Bless all those in trouble of any kind; and bless each one
of us.

St Patrick's Prayer

      Christ be with me, Christ within me,
      Christ before me, Christ beside me.
          Christ to win me,
      Christ to comfort and restore me,
      Christ beneath me, Christ above me,
      Christ in quiet, Christ in danger,
      Christ in hearts of all that love me,
      Christ in mouth of friend and stranger.

The Blessing

The grace of the Lord Jesus Christ be with us all. Amen.

TO LIVE AS WE OUGHT

A Prayer of George Adam Smith for use before reading the Bible

Almighty and most merciful God, who hast given the Bible to be the revelation of thy great love to man, and of thy power and will to save him; grant that our study of it may not be made vain by the callousness or carelessness of our hearts, but that by it we may be confirmed in penitence, lifted to hope, made strong for service, and above all filled with the true knowledge of thee and of thy Son Jesus Christ. Amen.

The Reading Lesson: 1 Timothy 6.3-16

Prayer

O God, tomorrow we go back to the world and to all its work and its activities. We remember that Jesus prayed, not that his friends should be taken out of the world, but that they should be kept from the evil of the world. Help us to live in this world as we ought to live.

Help us

To do the world's work faithfully and well;

To enjoy the world's pleasures wisely and temperately;

To value the world's goods, without becoming enslaved by them and without despising them;

To resist the world's temptations bravely and resolutely;

Always to remember that the greatest importance of the world is that it is the school and the training-ground for the still greater life which some day we shall live.

Help us to live in the world, not as those whose interests never look beyond the horizons of the world, but as those who always remember that in you we live and move and have our being, and that we are pledged to follow in the footsteps of our Lord and Master Jesus Christ.

A Prayer of Robert Louis Stevenson

Give us courage and gaiety and the quiet mind. Spare us to our friends, soften us to our enemies. Bless us, if it may be, in all our innocent endeavours. If it may not, give us strength to encounter that which is to come, that we may be brave in peril, constant in tribulation, temperate in wrath, and in all changes of fortune, and, down even to the gates of death, loyal and loving to one another: through Jesus Christ our Lord. Amen.

The Blessing

The Lord preserve our going out and our coming in, from this time forth for evermore. Amen.

THE WORLD GOD LOVES

The Opening Prayer

Give us this night, O God,
>> The hearing ear;
>> The understanding mind;
>> The resolute will,

that we may be,
>> Willing to listen to your word;
>> Able to grasp its meaning for us;
>> And strong to do it throughout the days of the
>> week:

through Jesus Christ our Lord. Amen.

The Reading Lesson: John 3.1-17

Prayer

Let us pray not only for ourselves but for the whole world which God so loved.

O God, send peace upon earth, that the nations no longer may prepare for war, and that they may try, not to destroy, but to understand each other.

O God, bless those parts of the world where people are learning the meaning of freedom and of liberty, and where new nations are being born. Take away all bitterness and hatred, and grant that those of all colours and races may learn to live in fellowship together.

O God, bless those places in the world where the name of Jesus is not known, or where it is rejected. Strengthen and uphold all missionaries in the peril and the loneliness of their task; and bring quickly the day when all people will confess that Jesus Christ is Lord.

O God, bless those parts of the world where people are homeless and hungry, and grant that those of us who have may ever be ready to share their plenty with those who have too little.

O God, bless those nations who have a different political creed and a different way of life from ours; and save us from being too quick to condemn that which we do not understand just because it is different, and help all people to find a fellowship in Jesus Christ which will cross all creeds and frontiers and weld them into one.

And help us to work, and to pray, and to give, and to sacrifice to bring the day when the kingdoms of the world will be the Kingdom of the Lord: through Jesus Christ our Lord. Amen.

The Prayer of the House of Commons

(This prayer is used at every sitting of the House of Commons. It was originally composed by Sir Christopher Yelverton, MP for Northampton, about the year 1578.)

Almighty God, by whom kings reign and princes decree justice, and from whom alone cometh all counsel, wisdom and understanding. We, thine unworthy servants, here gathered together in thy name, do most humbly beseech thee to send down the heavenly wisdom from above, to direct and guide us in all our consultations.

And grant that we, having thy fear always before our eyes, and laying aside all private interests, prejudices and partial affections, the result of all our counsels may be the glory of thy blessed name, the maintenance of true religion and justice, the safety, honour, and happiness of the Queen, the public welfare, peace and tranquillity of the realm, and the uniting and knitting together of the hearts of all persons and estates within the same in true Christian love and charity towards one another: through Jesus Christ our Lord and Saviour. Amen.

The Blessing

May the God of all grace, who has called us into his eternal glory by Christ Jesus, make us perfect, stablish, strengthen, settle us; to whom be glory and dominion for ever and ever. Amen.

THE WAY TO TRUE WEALTH

The Opening Prayer

O God,

> You are King; help us to come to you in loyal allegiance;
>
> You are Judge; help us to come to you in heartfelt sorrow for the wrong that we have done;
>
> You are Father; help us to come to you in confident and loving trust;
>
> You are God; help us to come to you in humble reverence and adoration.

Hear this our prayer: through Jesus Christ our Lord. Amen.

The Reading Lesson: Luke 12.13-21

Prayer

Help us, O God, to set our hearts only on the things which make life truly rich;

> Knowledge and skill which will make us able to make a real contribution to the world's work;
>
> Character which will make everyone able to trust us and to rely on us;
>
> Friends who will always be true to us.

To that end give us

> The diligence which will never shirk the toil of learning;
>
> The discipline which will make us refuse the easy way in order to train ourselves in goodness;
>
> The loyalty which will never let anyone down.

264

Forgive us
> If we have been lazy in learning and far slower than we need have been;
>
> If we have been careless in living and far more self-indulgent than we should have been;
>
> If we have been disloyal in friendship and far less faithful than we should have been.

Help us from now on
> To use to the full every gift and talent you have given us;
>
> To overcome every weakness which has us in its grip;
>
> To be forever true to you and to our friends and loved ones, no matter what the cost.

A Prayer of St Thomas Aquinas

God of all goodness, grant unto us to desire ardently, to seek wisely, to know surely, and to accomplish perfectly thy holy will, for the glory of thy name. Amen.

The Blessing

The grace of the Lord Jesus Christ go with us all. Amen.

THAT WE MAY BE AN EXAMPLE
TO ALL

The Opening Prayer

O God, our Father, bless us as we come to you this night.

> As pilgrims on the way we come to you for guidance for our road;
>
> As soldiers of the King we come to you for strength for the battle;
>
> As disciples of the Master we come to you for knowledge in our ignorance;
>
> As ambassadors of Christ we come to you for grace to make us good advertisements for our faith and for our Church.

This night we look to you for help for every need: through Jesus Christ our Lord. Amen.

The Reading Lesson: Matthew 7.13-20

Prayer

Help us, O God, to rid ourselves of all the things which keep us from being good examples of the faith which we profess.

Help us

> Never to demand standards from others which we never even attempt to live up to ourselves;
>
> Never to contradict with our lives that which we say with our lips;
>
> Never to be one thing to people's face and another behind their back.

Help us

> Never to make a promise and then to break it because it is difficult to keep;
>
> Never to do anything dishonourable, either to avoid trouble or to make gain;
>
> Never to be disloyal to a friend or untrue to a loved one.

Help us

> Never to teach or to persuade anyone to do a wrong thing;
>
> Never to give an example which will make it easier for someone else to go wrong;
>
> Never to laugh at anyone else's beliefs, and never to hide our own.

Help us to live that we shall never bring disgrace to ourselves, heartbreak to others, or grief to you.

An Ancient Prayer from the Gregorian Sacramentary

Go before us, O Lord, in all our doings with thy most gracious favour, and further us with thy continual help; that in all our works, begun, continued, and ended in thee, we may glorify thy holy name, and finally by thy mercy obtain everlasting life: through Jesus Christ our Lord. Amen.

The Blessing

The grace of the Lord Jesus Christ, the love of God, the fellowship of the Holy Spirit be upon us and upon all whom we love here and everywhere, and stay with each one of us and them this night and always.   Amen.

FOR THOSE IN DISTRESS

The Opening Prayer

O God, our Father, as we worship you this night, make us
      Humble enough to know that we need you;
      Wise enough to understand what you will say to us;
      Obedient enough to go out and to obey your com-
        mands: through Jesus Christ our Lord. Amen.

The Reading Lesson: Luke 4.33-40

Prayer

Lord Jesus, when you were on earth, they brought the sick
to you and you healed them all. This night we ask you to
bless all those in sickness, in weakness and in pain.

    Those who are blind and who cannot see the light of the
      sun, the beauty of the world, or the faces of their
      friends;
    Those who are deaf and who cannot hear the voices which
      speak to them;
    Those who are helpless and who must lie in bed while
      others go out and in:
        Bless all such.

    Those whose minds have lost their reason;
    Those who are so nervous that they cannot cope with life;
    Those who worry about everything:
        Bless all such.

    Those who must face life under some handicap;
    Those whose weakness means that they must always be
      careful;

> Those who are lame and maimed and who cannot enter
> into any of the strenuous activities or pleasures of life;
> Those who have been crippled by accident, or by illness,
> or who were born with a weakness of body or mind;
> Bless all such.

Grant that we in our health and our strength may never find those who are weak and handicapped a nuisance, but grant that we may always do and give all that we can to help them, and to make life easier for them.

An Ancient Prayer from the Gelasian Sacramentary

Lord God, Light of the minds that know thee, Life of the souls that love thee, Strength of the thoughts that seek thee; help us so to know thee that we may truly love thee, and so to love thee that we may fully serve thee, whose service is perfect freedom: through Jesus Christ our Lord. Amen.

The Blessing

God Almighty bless us with his Holy Spirit: guard us in our going out and coming in; keep us ever steadfast in his faith, free from sin, and safe from danger: through Jesus Christ our Lord. Amen.

IN TEMPTATION

The Opening Prayer

Give us this night, O God, as we worship you,

> Your truth to tell us what we ought to believe and what we ought to do;
>
> Your strength to make us able to face the things which by ourselves we cannot do;
>
> Your love that we may love you as you have first loved us, and that we may love our fellow men and women as you love them:

Through Jesus Christ our Lord. Amen.

The Reading Lesson: Luke 4.1-13

Prayer

Lord Jesus, you were tempted; help us when we are tempted.

When we are tempted, help us,

> Always to remember those who love us and trust us and believe in us, and whose hearts would be broken if we brought disgrace upon ourselves;
>
> Never to do anything which would bring us regret, remorse and shame to follow it;
>
> Never to do anything which we would have to hide, and about which we should be ashamed that others should know;
>
> Never to do anything which would injure anyone else;
>
> Always to remember that whatever we say or do you hear and see it.

Save us from ever being carried away by the heat or the impulse or the passion of the moment, and so forgetting the consequences of the thing we do.

Help us never to disobey our conscience and never to do anything which would take away our own self-respect.

Help us to make
Our pleasure such that we would never wish to hide it;
Our work such that we never need to be ashamed of it;
Our conduct to others such that we will never regret it.

At all times keep
Our thoughts pure and our words true;
Our actions honourable and our bodies clean.

Help us so to live that we can take everything in life and show it to you.

An Ancient Prayer

O heavenly Father, in whom we live and move and have our being, we humbly pray thee so to govern and guide us by thy Holy Spirit, that in all the cares and occupations of our daily life we may never forget thee, but remember that we are ever walking in thy sight: through Jesus Christ our Lord. Amen.

The Blessing

From the rising of the sun to the going down of the same, of thy goodness give us, with thy love inspire us, by thy Spirit guide us, by thy power protect us, and in thy mercy receive us, now and ever. Amen.

THE GOLDEN RULE

The Opening Prayer

Be with us, O God, tonight as we worship you,
>To teach us what we ought to know;
>To tell us what we ought to do;
>To make us what we ought to be.

This we ask for your love's sake.   Amen.

The Reading Lesson: Matthew 7.1-13

Prayer

Help us, O God, at all times to act towards others as we would wish them to act towards us.

Help us,
>To make the same allowances for others as we would wish them to make for us;
>To be as sympathetic and understanding to others as we would wish them to be to us;
>To encourage others as we would wish them to encourage us;
>To help others as we would wish them to help us;
>To be as just and fair to others as we would wish them to be to us;
>To forgive others as we would wish them to forgive us.

Before we criticize others, help us to remember what it feels like to be criticized.

Before we find fault with others, help us to remember what it feels like to be found fault with.

Before we condemn others, help us to remember what it feels like to be condemned.

272

Help us at all times to be like Jesus,
>Who went about doing good;
>Who was among us as one who serves;
>Who even on the Cross prayed that his enemies
>should be forgiven.

An Evening Prayer from the Book of Common Prayer

Lighten our darkness, we beseech thee, O Lord; and by thy great mercy defend us from all perils and dangers of this night: for the love of thy only Son, our Saviour, Jesus Christ. Amen.

The Blessing

May the blessing of God Almighty, the Father, the Son and the Holy Spirit, rest upon us and upon all our work and worship done in his name. May he give us light to guide us, courage to support us, and love to unite us, now and for evermore. Amen.

FOR THOSE WE LOVE

The Opening Prayer

Lord Jesus, Light of the World, give us your light;
>Light to help us to see the truth;
>Light to help us to see the way we ought to go;
>Light to see ourselves as we are;
>Light to see you in all your majesty and your love.

This we ask through Jesus Christ our Lord. Amen.

The Reading Lesson: Psalm 8

Prayer

O God, our Father, we ask you to bless those whom we love and those who are specially dear to us.

Bless our families, and help us to live in such a way that we may never bring anxiety or sorrow to them.

Bless our friends, and help us to live in such a way that we may never fail them and never let them down.

Bless those whom we love, and help us to live in such a way that we may never be untrue, unfaithful or disloyal to them.

Bless those whom we love and from whom we are separated, those whom work and duty have taken to other towns and other countries, and to sea, and at all times keep us true to them and keep them true to us, and grant that distance may never make us forget them, until we and they meet again.

Bless those who are,
>Ill and in pain;
>Sad and in loneliness;
>Poor and in need;

Worried and in distress;
Discouraged and in despair;
Tempted and in danger.

Bless all missionaries and especially those who bring the messages of your love to lands where there are strife and tension because new nations are being born.

A Prayer of Christina Rossetti

O Lord God of time and eternity, who makest us creatures of time that, when time is over, we may attain thy blessed eternity; with time, thy gift, give us also wisdom to redeem the time, lest our hour of grace be lost: for our Lord Jesus' sake. Amen.

The Blessing

The grace of the Lord Jesus Christ be on us all now, and stay with each one of us always. Amen.

FOR VICTORY OVER TEMPTATION

The Opening Prayer

Give us tonight, O God,

> Humility to listen to your word,
> Wisdom to understand your word;
> Obedience to attempt your word;
> Strength to obey your word:

through Jesus Christ our Lord who is the Word.   Amen.

The Reading Lesson: Luke 9.57-62

Prayer

O God, our Father, give us strength to defeat the temptations which so often attack us.

> Help us in spite of all seductions to sin to keep our bodies chaste and pure.
> Help us in spite of all inducements to pride to keep our minds humble and ever learning.
> Help us in spite of all the invitations to give them to the wrong things to give our hearts only to the things which are honourable, and above all to you.

Keep us,

> From the self-indulgence and the lack of self-control which can ruin life for ourselves and for others;
> From the mental lethargy and laziness which will not make the effort to learn;
> From all wrong desires and all mistaken loyalties which will make us give our hearts to the wrong things.

And help us to love you so much that we will hate the sins which grieve you.

A Prayer of John Baillie

Give me an open ear, O God, that I may hear thy voice calling me to high endeavour. Too often have I been deaf to the appeals thou hast addressed to me, but now give me courage to answer, Here am I, send me. And when any one of thy children, my human brothers, cries out in need, give me an open ear to hear in that cry thy call to service. Amen.

The Blessing

The peace of God which passeth all understanding, keep our hearts and minds in the knowledge and love of God, and of his Son Jesus Christ our Lord, and the blessing of God Almighty, the Father, the Son and the Holy Spirit, be amongst us and remain with us always. Amen.

FOR THE HELP OF GOD

The Opening Prayer

Give us this night, O God,

    The gratitude which really wants to thank you;

    The penitence which really wishes to tell you that it is sorry;

    The sense of need which really makes us come to you for the things which you alone can give;

    The obedience which will really make us listen and obey.

Hear and answer this our prayer, through Jesus Christ our Lord. Amen.

The Reading Lesson: Matthew 7.21-28

Prayer

O God, our Father, we ask your help so to live that we shall always be on the right way.

    Guide us in every choice which life brings to us,

        so that we may always choose the right way.

    Purify all our ambitions,

        so that we may set our hearts only on the things which please you.

    Control all our thoughts,

        that they may never linger on the wrong things, or stray down the pathways in which they ought not to go.

    Guard our lips,

        so that no word which would shame ourselves or hurt another may ever pass through them.

Direct our actions, so that we may always work with diligence, act in honour, and live in kindness.

And help us not only to ask for your help but also always to be willing to accept it when you offer it to us, so that we may stop wanting our own way and begin to take yours.

A Prayer of John Knox

Let thy mighty hand, O Lord our God, and outstretched arm be our defence; thy mercy and loving kindness in Jesus Christ, thy dear Son, our salvation; thy all-true word, our instruction; the grace of thy life-giving Spirit our comfort and consolation, to the end and in the end. Amen.

The Closing Prayer

Lord Jesus, teach us to love thee and to abide with thee in the love of the Father and the fellowship of the Holy Spirit, now and ever. Amen.

PENITENCE, PETITION, AND GRATITUDE

The Opening Prayer

Help us, O God, not to grudge these few minutes when we worship you.

Help us not to regard them as just a formality or a duty to perform.

Help us tonight really to listen for your voice, and really to speak to you, so that we may go out to make life better than it has ever been before: through Jesus Christ our Lord. Amen.

The Reading Lesson: Proverbs 8.12-21

Prayer

O God, we need your forgiveness.

> For the failure to do what we know is right;
>
> For the failure to love and to forgive and to serve others as we know we ought to do;
>
> For the failure to be what we can be and to do what we can do:
>> Forgive us, O God.

O God, we need your help,

> Help not so much to know what is right—we know that already—but help to do what is right;
>
> Help to resist the temptations which come to us from inside ourselves and from the invitations and the persuasions of others;
>
> Help not to be afraid to do the right thing;
>
> Help to be what we can be and to do what we can do:
>> Give us this help, O God.

O God, we owe you thanks.

    Thanks for our health and our strength;

    Thanks for all the things we enjoy and for all the people who are dear to us;

    Thanks for giving us life and for giving us everything that makes life so gloriously worthwhile;

    Thanks for Jesus our Saviour and Friend:

Send us out from this place to show our gratitude by the faithfulness of our lives.

A Prayer of Dean Vaughan

O Lord God, give us grace to set a good example to all amongst whom we live, to be just and true in all our dealings, to be strict and conscientious in the discharge of every duty, pure and temperate in all enjoyment, kind and charitable and courteous towards all men; that so the mind of Jesus Christ may be formed in us, and all men may take knowledge of us that we are his disciples: through Jesus Christ our Lord. Amen.

The Blessing

The love of God, the grace of our Lord Jesus Christ, the fellowship of the Holy Spirit be with us all. Amen.

GRATITUDE AND PENITENCE

The Opening Prayer

O God, our Father, grant that this short time of worship may not be to us a nuisance and something with which we really cannot be bothered. Grant that it may not be a mere formality which has to be pushed through because it is the custom. Give us tonight hearts which really want to tell you of their gratitude for your gifts and of their sorrow for their mistakes. And make us to come with gladness, to wait with expectation, and to worship with concentration this night: through Jesus Christ our Lord.   Amen.

The Reading Lesson: Isaiah 55.1-11

Prayer

O God, our Father, we bring you thanks this night for all the gifts which you have given to us.

We thank you
    That you have made us alive;
    That you have given us this fair world to live in;
    That you have given us healthy bodies and sane minds;
    That you have given us work to do and leisure to enjoy;
    That you have surrounded us with friends to delight in
        and dear ones to love;
    That you have given us Jesus as our Master, our Sa-
        viour, and our Lord.

O God, our Father, we bring you this night our sorrow for all the wrong things we have done.

Forgive us,
    For our failure to work as we ought to work, and to
        study as we ought to study;

For our failure to forgive as we ought to forgive, and
to be kind as we ought to be kind;
For the failure to be true to our friends, to be loyal to
our loved ones, to be faithful and obedient to you;
For our failure to do what we know we ought to do,
and to be what we know we ought to be.

Help us in the days to come to show the reality of our
gratitude by living more nearly as we ought.

A Prayer of George Matheson

O Divine Spirit, who in all the events of life art knocking
at the door of my heart, help me to respond to thee. I would
not be driven blindly as the stars over their courses. I would
not be made to work out thy will unwillingly, to fulfil thy
law unintelligently, to obey thy mandates unsympathetically.
I would take the events of my life as good and perfect gifts
from thee; I would receive even the sorrows of life as dis-
guised gifts from thee. I would have my heart open at all
times to receive—at morning, noon, and night; in spring and
summer and winter. Whether thou comest to me in sunshine
or in rain, I would take thee into my heart joyfully. Thou
art thyself more than the sunshine; thou art thyself com-
pensation for the rain; it is thee, and not thy gifts, I crave;
knock and I shall open unto thee.   Amen.

The Blessing

The grace of the Lord Jesus Christ be with us all.   Amen.

TO KEEP LIFE HAPPY

The Opening Prayer

Grant, O God, that here tonight in the light of your presence, and in comparison with Jesus, we may see our lives as they are and life as it ought to be. Give us true sorrow for our failure to be what we ought to be, and then give us the strength and the determination to be what you mean us to be: through Jesus Christ our Lord. Amen.

The Reading Lesson: Luke 20.19-26

Prayer

O God, keep us from the things which are bound to make life unhappy.

Keep us from
> The eyes which can always find some fault to see;
> The tongue which can always find something to grumble about;
> The heart which can always find some grudge and some bitterness to cherish.

Keep us from
> The perverseness which does not want anything it gets, and which always wants what it has not got;
> The ingratitude which does not even realize what it is getting;
> The attitude of mind which lives in continual resentment.

Give us
> The even temper which can take things as they come;
> The sense of humour which can always find some cause to smile;

284

The gratitude which can always find something for
which to be thankful;
The cheerfulness which not all earth's shadows and dis-
appointments can extinguish.

Give us the spirit which can enjoy life, and which can help
others to enjoy it.

A Prayer of D. L. Moody

Use me then, my Saviour, for whatever purpose, and in
whatever way, thou mayest require. Here is my poor heart,
an empty vessel; fill it with thy grace. Here is my sinful
and troubled soul; quicken it and refresh it with thy love.
Take my heart for thine abode; my mouth to spread abroad
the glory of thy name; my love and all my powers for the
advancement of thy believing people; and never suffer the
steadfastness and confidence of my faith to waver—that so
at all times I may be enabled from the heart to say, Jesus
needs me, and I him.   Amen.

The Blessing

The Lord bless us and keep us. The Lord make his face
shine upon us and be gracious unto us. The Lord lift up
his countenance upon us and give us peace.   Amen.

THE IDEAL AND THE WAY TO IT

The Opening Prayer

Lord Jesus, you are the Way, the Truth and the Life. Help us tonight,

> To see more clearly the way we ought to take;
> To know more fully the truth we ought to know;
> To go out to live more faithfully the life we ought to live.

This we ask for your love's sake. Amen.

The Reading Lesson: Luke 11.1-13

Prayer

Eternal and ever-blessed God, equip us, not only to see, but also to attain, the ideal.

Grant unto us,

> The wisdom to know what is right, and the courage to do it;
> The clear sight to see the right way, and the perseverance to walk in it;
> The vision to see the ideal, and the discipline to toil towards it.

Help us never to be satisfied

> With words without deeds;
> With plans without performance;
> With schemes without results;
> With dreams without toil to make the dream come true.

Teach us

> That the way to the stars is always steep;
> That sweat is the price of all things precious;
> That there never can be any crown without a cross.

So make us willingly to spend life that we may gain life, and to take up our cross and follow in the footsteps of our Lord and Master, Jesus Christ.

A Prayer of Benjamin Jenks

O Lord, renew our spirits and draw our hearts unto thyself, that our work may not be to us a burden, but a delight; and give us such a mighty love to thee as may sweeten all our obedience. O, let us not serve thee with the spirit of bondage as slaves, but with the cheerfulness and gladness of children, delighting ourselves in thee and rejoicing in thy work. Amen.

The Blessing

The grace of our Lord Jesus Christ, the love of God, and the fellowship of the Holy Spirit be upon us all this night and stay with each one of us always. Amen.

FAILURE, SUCCESS, ROUTINE

The Opening Prayer

O God, our Father, tonight we come to you,

> To hear your word as the Bible is read;
> To sing your praise in the poetry and the music of our hymns;
> To speak to you in our prayers;
> To listen to you in our silence.

Help us tonight to worship you in spirit and in truth: through Jesus Christ our Lord. Amen.

The Reading Lesson: John 15.1-14

Prayer

O God, our Father, we ask you tonight specially to bless those who feel that they have failed:

> Those who have fallen to temptation,
>> and who regret it;
> Those who have hurt their loved ones,
>> and who are ashamed of it;
> Those who have failed in some task,
>> and who know that it is their own fault.

We ask you tonight specially to bless those who have succeeded:

> Those who have done well,
>> that they may be kept from pride;
> Those who are happy and carefree,
>> that they may never feel that they can do without you;
> Those who feel that there is nothing to worry about,
>> that over-confidence may not bring them disaster.

We ask you to bless those for whom life is very ordinary:
   Those who feel that nothing ever happens;
   Those who feel that life is dull and uninteresting;
   Those who are bored and fed up with the routine of
   everyday.
         Teach all such that it is in the common tasks they
         find or miss their destiny and their reward.

You know us better than we know ourselves. Bless us, not
as we ask, but as you in your wisdom know that we need.

A Prayer of J. H. Jowett

O God, keep me sensitive to the grace that is round about
me. May the familiar not become neglected! May I see thy
goodness in my daily bread, and may the comfort of my
home take my thoughts to the mercy seat of God! Amen.

The Blessing

May grace, mercy and peace from Father, Son and Holy
Spirit, one God, rest on and abide with each one of us now
and for evermore. Amen.

THE USE OF LIFE

The Opening Prayer

We come to you tonight, O God, because we need you.

    We cannot work well by day without your help, and we
        cannot sleep well at night without your blessing.

We come to you tonight, O God, because we love you.

    We want to speak to you and we want to listen to you
        speaking to us before the day ends and the night comes.

So come to meet us as we have come to meet you: through
Jesus Christ our Lord.   Amen.

The Reading Lesson: Colossians 3.16—4.6

Prayer

O God, help us to think of life as we ought to think of it,
and to use life as it ought to be used.

Help us always to remember,

       That you gave us life,

            and that it is not ours to do with as we like;

       That life comes to an end,

            and that we must not waste it when we have it;

       That we cannot tell what a day will bring to us,

            and so we must not put things off until tomorrow
            in case tomorrow never comes.

Help us,

       To use life wisely and not foolishly;

       To use life generously and not selfishly;

       To use life strenuously and not lazily;

       To use life with discipline and not with self-indulgence;

       To use life in the constant memory that one day we
           shall give account of it to you.

To that end help us always to walk with Jesus who is the Lord of all good life and who came to give us life and life more abundantly.

A Prayer of Thomas à Kempis

O Lord, thou knowest what is best for us, let this or that be done as thou shalt please. Give what thou wilt, and how much thou wilt, and when thou wilt. Deal with me as thou thinkest good, and as best pleaseth thee. Set me where thou wilt and deal with me in all things as thou wilt. Behold, I am thy servant, prepared for all things; for I desire not to live unto myself, but unto thee; and O that I could do it worthily and perfectly! Amen.

The Blessing

The blessing of God, Father, Son and Holy Spirit, be with us all now and stay with each one of us always. Amen.

The Opening Prayer

O God, the Father,

>   make us sure this night of the power which has
>   created us, and of the love which always sustains us.

O Jesus Christ, the Son,

>   make us sure this night of the love which died for
>   us and of the risen presence which is with us now,
>   always and to the end of the world.

O Holy Spirit, the Helper,

>   make us sure this night that you will teach us what
>   we ought to say, what we ought to do, where we
>   ought to go, if we ask your help in faith and accept
>   it in obedience.

And to Father, Son, and Holy Spirit be all the honour and
all the glory, world without end.   Amen.

The Reading Lesson: Psalm 121

Prayer

O God, tonight we specially ask you to help us never to
allow the great things of life to go wrong.

Help us never to allow

>   Caution to become cowardice,
>
>   or courage to become recklessness.

Help us never to allow

>   Carefulness to become meanness,
>
>   or spending to become squandering.

Help us never to allow

>   Honesty to become discourtesy,
>
>   or politeness to become evasion of the truth.

Help us never to allow
>Liberty to become licence,
>or pleasure to become sin.

Help us never selfishly to make use of our friends, never thoughtlessly to take our loved ones for granted, never to make your love an excuse for thinking that we can do what we like. Help us always to remember how we have been loved and to try to be more worthy of it.

A Prayer for the Tongue

Set a watch upon our tongue, O Lord, that we may never speak the cruel word which is untrue; or, being true, is not the whole truth; or, being wholly true, is merciless; for the love of Jesus Christ our Lord. Amen.

The Blessing

The Lord preserve our going out and our coming in from this time forth for evermore. Amen.

BODY, MIND AND SPIRIT

The Opening Prayer

O be with us, gracious Father,
While before thy feet we bow;
Let the angel of thy presence
Hover o'er thy temple now.
Hear this our prayer, through Jesus Christ our Lord. Amen.

The Reading Lesson: Romans 12.1, 2, 9-21

Prayer

O God, our Father, you have made us body, mind and spirit. Help us to make each part of ourselves what it ought to be.

You have given us bodies.
Help us to keep them in health. Grant that we may never find pleasure in any habit or indulgence which would injure our bodies. Help us to keep them fit, and make us willing to accept the discipline which will keep them from becoming flabby and unhealthy.

You have given us minds.
Help us to study to fit ourselves for the trade, the craft, the profession by which one day we will make a living for ourselves and for those we love. Keep us from the lazy mind which will not learn, and from the shut mind that cannot learn. Help us every day to enrich our minds by adding some new thing to our store of knowledge.

You have given us spirits.
Help us to remember that there is a bit of us which will always go on, that there is a part of us which can speak

294

to you, and to which you can speak. Help us to remember that we are creatures of eternity as well as of time; and so in this world help us to fit ourselves for the life into which we will one day enter.

A Prayer for the Compassion of Christ

O Lord Jesus, who wast moved with compassion for all who had gone astray, with indignation for all who suffered wrong: inflame our hearts with the burning fire of thy love, that with thee we may seek out the lost, with thee have mercy on the fallen, and with thee stand fast for truth and righteousness, both now and always. Amen. (E. Milner-White and G. W. Briggs.)

The Blessing

The blessing of God the Father, the Son and the Holy Spirit, be on us all now and stay with each one of us always. Amen.

THE CLEANSING OF SELFISHNESS

The Opening Prayer

O God, our Father, make us for this time of worship very conscious and very aware of your presence.

Help us to remember your holiness, that there may be reverence in our hearts.

Help us to remember your love that we may be quite sure that you are the Father who is ready to welcome all who come to him: through Jesus Christ our Lord. Amen.

The Reading Lesson: Psalm 95.1-6

Prayer

O Lord Jesus, you have taught us that, if we wish to follow you, we must leave self behind. Keep us from all selfishness in our lives.

Keep us from being selfish in our aims and our ambitions,
and help us to seek always to serve and never to rule.

Keep us from being selfish in the use of the gifts and the possessions which you have given to us,
and help us always to give and to share, and never to keep and to hold.

Keep us from being selfish in our pleasures,
and help us never to find pleasure in anything which would hurt another.

Keep us from being selfish in our treatment of other people, from being careless of their feelings, unsympathetic to their troubles, regardless of their convenience, from making use of them to suit ourselves.
and help us always to think of others as much as we think of ourselves.

Help us to find our pleasure in helping others, our happiness in making others happy, our joy in, like our Master, going about doing good.

An unknown Saint's Evening Prayer

O God, who hast drawn over the weary day the restful veil of night, enfold us in thy heavenly peace. Lift from our hands our tasks, and all through the night bear in thy bosom the full weight of our burdens and sorrows, that in untroubled slumber we may press our weariness close to thy strength, and win new power for the morrow's duties from thee who givest to thy beloved in sleep: through Jesus Christ our Lord. Amen.

The Blessing

Now unto him that is able to do exceedingly abundantly above all that we ask or think, be glory in the Church throughout all ages world without end; and may the blessing of God, Father, Son and Holy Spirit be on us all now and stay with each one of us this night and always. Amen.

THAT WE MAY LIVE LIFE WELL

The Opening Prayer

> Grant us thy truth to make us free,
>> And kindling hearts to burn for thee;
> Till all thy holy altars claim,
>> One heavenly light, one holy flame.

O God, our Father, give us this night the light of thy truth in our minds and the fire of thy love in our hearts: through Jesus Christ our Lord. Amen.

The Reading Lesson: Micah 6.6-8

Prayer

O God, you have given us life. Help us to live in such a way that we shall make the contribution to life which we ought to make.

Keep us from living ungratefully,
> And help us always to remember all that has been done for us and all that we have received.

Keep us from living irresponsibly,
> And help us always to remember that we shall one day answer to you for the way in which we have used everything which you have given to us.

Keep us from living carelessly,
> And grant that we may never bring shame to ourselves or hurt and sorrow to others because we did not stop to think.

Keep us from living selfishly,
> And grant that our comfort, our pleasure, our wishes, our aims, our ambitions may not be the only things which matter to us. Help us to remember that we have

received our time, our talents and our money to use not only for ourselves, but also for our fellow men and women.
Keep us from living dangerously,
And grant that we may never foolishly flirt with temptation or play with fire. Help us to have nothing to do with the things and the pleasures which we know are wrong.
Keep us from living unsocially,
And help us to take our full part in the life and the work and the service of the community.
Keep us from living exclusively,
And grant that we may never shut any one out from our society because of colour, party, or creed.

A Homegoing Prayer

Grant us thy peace upon our homeward way;
With thee began, with thee shall end the day.
Guard thou the lips from sin, the hearts from shame,
Which in this house have called upon thy name.

The Blessing

The blessing of God, Father, Son and Holy Spirit, be on us and remain with us all.   Amen.

OUR CHURCH, OUR COUNTRY, AND OUR WORLD

The Opening Prayer

Jesus, stand among us
In thy risen power;
Let this time of worship
Be a hallowed hour.

Lord Jesus, help us this night indeed to feel that you are here. This we ask for your love's sake. Amen.

The Reading Lesson: I Timothy 2.1-7

Prayer

Tonight in our prayers let us send our thoughts out beyond ourselves and beyond our fellowship into the wider world.

First of all, let us pray for the Church

O God, our Father, bless your Church. What in her is dark, illumine; what is low, raise and support; what is wanting, supply; what is in error, take away. Make her here and all over the world a real fellowship in which there are no quarrels and no divisions, no distinctions of race or colour, of class or party, a fellowship in which all are really one. And help us in our church to work and to pray to make the Church like that.

Now let us pray for our country

O God, our Father, help us to love our country with a passion so strong and so true that we shall be jealous for its honour and instant in its service, and that we shall not rest until we have made this a land where men and women walk in the freedom of the truth and in the light of knowledge. To that end help us to find leaders whose only master is their conscience and who ever speak with you before they speak to others.

Now let us pray for the whole world

O God, who made of one blood all nations who dwell in the world, bless this world. Bring quickly the day when colour and race shall no longer divide us. Give your help in those places where new nations are being born, and grant that bitterness and hatred may not destroy brotherhood and peace. And hasten the time when the knowledge of yourself will cover the earth as the waters cover the sea and when people shall no longer even speak of war.

A Prayer of Saint Bernard

O Jesus, ever with us stay,
Make all our moments calm and bright;
Chase the dark night of sin away,
Shed o'er the world thine own true light.

The Blessing

The grace of the Lord Jesus Christ be with us all. Amen.

THE PEACE OF GOD

The Opening Prayer

The Psalmist thanked God that God had kept his feet from falling, his eyes from tears, and his soul from death. Let us ask God to do that for us.

Eternal and ever-blessed God, grant us,

The light and the guidance which keep our feet from falling;

The comfort and the consolation which will keep our eyes from tears;

The life eternal which will keep our souls from death: through Jesus Christ our Lord. Amen.

The Reading Lesson: Isaiah 11.1-9

A Prayer for Peace

O God, you are the God of peace; help us to find peace.

Help us to have peace in our own homes, and save us from the irritability, the selfishness, the bad temper which make us so difficult to live with.

Help us to have peace at our work. Take away the suspicion and distrust between employer and employee, and help all to find a way to live in a partnership for the common good.

Help us to have peace within the Church. Help us to get rid of the divisions between the different branches of the Church; and within our own congregations help us never to let anything disturb the friendship and the fellowship which should be there.

Help us to find peace between race and race. Help us never to dislike others and never to look down upon them because of their race or colour. Help us to see in everyone a brother or sister for whom Christ died.

Help us to find peace between nation and nation. Help us to see the folly of war and to realize that no nation can ever really win any war. Give to this and to every other country leaders who seek for peace, and help us not to rest until we have built up a civilization in which people shall never even speak of war.

King Charles the First's Prayer

O Lord, make the way plain before me. Let thy glory be my end, thy Word my rule; and then, thy will be done. Amen.

The Blessing

The grace of the Lord Jesus Christ be with us all.   Amen.

THAT WE MAY DO OUR DUTY

The Opening Prayer

Grant us, this night, O God, clear sight to see the way we ought to take, and courage and perseverance to follow it to the end. Give us humility to ask what is your will for us, and give us trust and obedience to say, Your will be done: through Jesus Christ our Lord. Amen.

The Reading Lesson: Psalm 96

Prayer

Help us, O God, to fulfil all the duties which life brings to us.

Help us,
>To honour our families;
>To be loyal to our friends;
>To be true to our loved ones.

Help us,
>To be diligent in our studies;
>To be conscientious in our work;
>To be wise in our pleasure.

Help us,
>To be brave in danger;
>To be strong in temptation;
>To be uncomplaining in pain;
>To be cheerful in disappointment.

Help us,
>To remain humble in prosperity;
>To remain hopeful in adversity.

And help us at all times so to live that our life and conduct may make it plain that we belong to you.

A Prayer of Rabindranath Tagore

Give us the strength lightly to bear our joys and sorrows.
Give us the strength to make our love fruitful in service.
Give us the strength never to disown the poor, or bend our
  knees before insolent might.
Give us the strength to raise our minds high above daily
  trifles.
And give us the strength to surrender our strength to thy
  will with love.   Amen.

The Blessing

May God, our heavenly Father, bless and keep us his children this night and for ever.   Amen.

THE THINGS WE OWE

The Opening Prayer

Grant, O God, that this night each of us may find in you
that which we need. Grant that

> The perplexed may find guidance;
> The tempted may find resistance power;
> The doubting may find certainty;
> The sad may find comfort;
> The lonely may find friendship.

Out of your all-sufficient grace supply our every need:
through Jesus Christ our Lord. Amen.

The Reading Lesson: Psalm 8

Prayer

Help us, O God, to give to all with whom we come into
contact that which we ought to give.

Help us to give to our families, care and affection.

Help us to give to those with whom we work, respect and
attention.

Help us to give to friends and to those who love us, our un-
failing loyalty.

Help us to give thanks to those who help us, and forgiveness
to those who hurt us.

Help us to share the joy of those who are happy, and the
sorrow of those who are sad.

Help us to help those whose work is hard, to praise those
who have done well, and to sympathize with those who
have failed.

A Prayer of J. H. Jowett

Grant that we may walk as Christ walked; grant that what the Spirit was in him, such he may be also in us; grant that our lives may be refashioned after the pattern of his life; grant that we may do today here on earth what Christ would have done, and in the way he would have done it; grant that we may become vessels of his grace, instruments of his will, to thy glory and honour: through Jesus Christ our Lord. Amen.

The Blessing

May God, the Fountain of all blessing, fill us with the understanding of sacred knowledge. May he keep us sound in faith, steadfast in hope, and persevering in patient charity. And may the blessing of the Father, the Son and the Holy Spirit, and the peace of the Lord be always with us. Amen.

FAITHFUL IN EVERYTHING

The Opening Prayer

O God, our Father, tonight we are here for this short time
to read your book and to pray. Help us,
> To study your Book. that we may understand what it has
> to say to us;
> To obey your Book, that we may be saved from all errors
> and mistakes;
> To trust your Book, that we may be able to go on and to
> meet anything that life will bring to us in courage and
> in hope.

This we ask for your love's sake.   Amen.

The Reading Lesson: Isaiah 58.1-12

Prayer

O God, you are the Lord of all good life; help us to be faithful in everything which you have given us to do.

Help us to be conscientious and honest in our work, that
nothing we do may be less than our best.

Help us to be diligent and careful in our study, that we
may be able to understand, to remember and to use that
which we read and discover.

Help us to be regular in our daily reading of your word,
that no day may pass without your Book being in our
hands.

Help us to be faithful in our attendance at church and
in fellowship, that we may find joy in worshipping and in
talking with others who are trying to follow Jesus.

Help us never to forget each day to pray, that we may begin,
continue and end each day in thinking of you.

So help us to make of life what you meant it to be.

Sir Thomas More's Prayer

Give us, O Lord, an humble, quiet, peaceable, patient, tender, and charitable mind, and in all our thoughts, words, and deeds a taste of thy Holy Spirit. Give us, O Lord, a lively faith, a firm hope, a fervent charity, a love of thee. Take from us all lukewarmness in meditation, dullness in prayer. Give us fervour and delight in thinking of thee and thy grace, thy tender compassion towards us. The things that we pray for, good Lord, give us grace to labour for: through Jesus Christ our Lord. Amen.

The Blessing

May the Lord lead us when we go, and keep us when we sleep, and talk with us when we wake; and may the peace of God, which passeth all understanding, keep our hearts and minds in Christ Jesus our Lord. Amen.

The Opening Prayer

Grant to us tonight, O God, the seeing eye, the hearing ear, the understanding mind and the loving heart, so that we may see your glory, and hear your word, and understand your truth, and answer to your love: through Jesus Christ our Lord. Amen.

The Reading Lesson: I Corinthians 1.18-31

Prayer

O God, touch every part of us with your Spirit and your power.

Be in our hearts, that every unclean and impure thought may be banished from them.

Be in our minds, that they may be eager to learn, adventurous to think, and retentive to remember.

Be in our eyes that they may never linger on any forbidden thing, or find delight in looking at that which is soiled.

Be in our ears that, above the many voices of the clamorous world, we may hear your still small voice speaking to us.

Be upon our hands, that we may do an honest day's work for ourselves and that we may ever help others.

Be upon our feet, that we may never stray from the way in which we ought to go.

So be on every part of us that we may be able to take all life and bring it as an offering to you.

An Evening Prayer

Almighty God, our heavenly Father, abide with us as the

day draws to its close. Grant us the peace of pardoned children, and the security of those who are at home in thy house, fed at thy table, comforted at thy knee, and guarded by thine unsleeping watch: for thy Name's sake. Amen.

The Blessing

The grace of our Lord Jesus Christ be with us all. Amen.

THE STRENGTH OF GOD

The Opening Prayer

Grant, O God, that we may never grudge any time that we give to you, but that we may always be,

Eager to hear your word;
Glad to sing your praise;
Ready to hear your truth;
Happy to pray to you.

This we ask through Jesus Christ our Lord.   Amen.

The Reading Lesson: Lamentations 3.22-27

Prayer

O God, Source of all strength and goodness,

Help us to resist the things which by ourselves we cannot resist,

To overcome the temptations which fascinate us;
To break the habits which enslave us;
To say No to anything which invites us to set foot on the wrong way.

Help us to do and to be all the things which by ourselves we cannot do and be.

We have never been as good as we could be;
We have never done anything as well as it could be done;
Life has never been what it might have been and could have been.

Give us the strength and wisdom to be what you meant us to be, and to do what you meant us to do, so that we may fulfil the purpose for which you sent us into this your world.

A Prayer of Charles Kingsley

Guide us, teach us, and strengthen us, O Lord, we beseech thee, until we become such as thou wouldst have us to be; pure, gentle, truthful, high-minded, courteous, generous, able, dutiful and useful: for thy honour and thy glory. Amen.

The Blessing

The love of God, the grace of our Lord Jesus Christ, the fellowship of the Holy Spirit be upon us, and upon all whom we love here and everywhere, and stay with each one of us and them this night and always.   Amen.

GOD'S CLEANSING POWER

The Opening Prayer

O God, you have shown us the more excellent way; help us always to walk in it.

> Restrain us when we are like to go astray;
> Refresh us when we are tired;
> Encourage us when we are depressed;
> Help us, when we fall, to rise and to begin again.

And so keep us in the way everlasting, until in your good time we reach our journey's end: through Jesus Christ our Lord. Amen.

The Reading Lesson: Proverbs 15.13-21

Prayer

O God, our Father, Giver of all purity and grace, cleanse and strengthen every part of us.

> Be on our lips that we may speak no false, no cruel, no ugly, no impure word.
>
> Be in our eyes that we may look not for things to criticize, but for things to praise, that our eyes may never linger on any forbidden thing, but ever look on the things which are beautiful and good.
>
> Be in our minds that they always be brave to think, eager to learn, and retentive to remember, and that all our thoughts may be pure.
>
> Be in our hearts, that we may always love that which is highest and best, and that we may surrender them in loyalty and in devotion to you.

A Prayer of Lancelot Andrewes

May the power of the Father govern us. May the wisdom of the Son enlighten us. May the operation of the Holy Spirit quicken us. O God, we beseech thee, guard our souls; sustain our bodies; exalt our senses; direct our course; regulate our manners; bless our undertakings; fulfil our petitions; inspire us with holy thoughts; pardon what is past; rectify what is present; order what is to come; and all for the sake of Jesus Christ our Lord and Saviour, who alone can make us perfect as he is perfect. Amen.

The Blessing

May grace, mercy and peace from Father, Son and Holy Spirit, one God, rest on us all now and remain with each one of us always. Amen.

FOR LOYALTY

The Opening Prayer

O God, our Father, grant that our meeting here together
with you tonight may make our lives

> Useful in service;
> Beautiful with love;
> Strong in faith;

so that we may go out to serve you and to serve our fellow-
men better than before: through Jesus Christ our Lord.
Amen.

The Reading Lesson: Ruth 1.1-18

Prayer

O God, you have made our hearts such that loyalty is the
most precious quality in this life. Help us to have this
loyalty.

> Help us to have loyalty to our principles, so that every-
> one may know where we stand and what we stand
> for.

> Help us to have loyalty to the truth, so that everyone
> may know that our word can be trusted absolutely.

> Help us to have loyalty to our friends, so that we will
> never let them down, and so that they can be certain
> that we will stand by them in any company and in
> any circumstances.

> Help us to be loyal to our loved ones and to be true to
> them through all the chances and the changes of this
> life.

316

Help us to be loyal to you, so that we will never be ashamed to show whose we are and whom we serve, and so that we shall be proud to let the world see that for us Jesus Christ is Lord.

A Prayer of Clement of Rome

We beseech thee, Lord and Master, to be our help and succour. Save those who are in tribulation; have mercy on the lonely; lift up the fallen; show thyself unto the needy; heal the ungodly; convert the wanderers of thy people; feed the hungry; raise up the weak; comfort the faint-hearted. Let all the peoples know that thou art God alone, and Jesus Christ is thy Son, and we are thy people and the sheep of thy pasture: for the sake of Christ Jesus. Amen.

The Blessing

The Lord bless us and keep us. The Spirit of the Lord cleanse and purify our inmost hearts, and enable us to shun all evil. The Lord enlighten our understandings and cause the Light of his Truth to shine into our hearts. The Lord fill us with faith and love towards him. The Lord be with us day and night, in our coming in and going out, in our sorrow and in our joy. And bring us at length into his eternal rest. Amen.

The Opening Prayer

Help us, O God, now and at all times,
> To respect ourselves;
> To love our fellow men and women;
> To reverence you;

that we may do nothing,
> To shame ourselves;
> To injure others;
> To grieve you:

through Jesus Christ our Lord. Amen.

The Reading Lesson: Proverbs 3.1-12

Prayer

O God, save us from being unwise enough to refuse the discipline which we ought to accept.

> Keep us from being too proud to ask for advice.
> Keep us from being too self-conceited to accept guidance.
> Keep us from being too self-willed to endure rebuke.
> Keep us from foolishly disregarding the experience of those who are older and wiser than we are.
> Keep us from the self-confidence that cannot believe that it can be wrong, and which can see no point of view but its own.

Make us wise enough to realize our own ignorance, and to recognize our own weakness, that we may come to you who are the source of all wisdom and all strength.

The Bedouin Camel-Drivers' Prayer at Sunset

O Lord, be gracious unto us! In all that we hear or see, in all that we say or do, be gracious unto us. I ask pardon of the Great God. I ask pardon at the sunset, when every sinner turns to him. Now and for ever I ask pardon of God. O Lord, cover us from our sins, guard our children, and protect our weaker friends.

The Blessing

May the Lord Jesus Christ fill us with spiritual joy, may his Spirit make us strong and tranquil in the truths of his promises. And may the blessing of the Lord come on us abundantly. Amen.

THAT WE MAY NOT SPOIL THINGS

The Opening Prayer

O God, our Father, help us to find here tonight the power which will inspire us to goodness and restrain us from sin. Help us to find forgiveness for all the wrong things that we have done in the past and strength and grace to do better in the future: through Jesus Christ our Lord. Amen.

The Reading Lesson: Matthew 6.1-5, 16-18

Prayer

O God, our Father, keep us from doing things in a way that takes all the value out of them.

Keep us from doing things unwillingly and with a grudge, in a way that makes it quite clear that the whole thing is a nuisance to us.

Keep us from doing things so badly and so inattentively that they have to be done all over again.

Keep us from doing things in such a hurry that they are only half done.

Keep us from doing things in order to show off how good and how kind and how clever we are.

Help us to do everything in such a way that we would be happy to know that you are watching us and glad to offer what we have done to you.

A Prayer of Archbishop Laud for the Church

Gracious Father, we humbly beseech thee for thy universal Church. Fill it with all truth, in all truth with all peace. Where it is corrupt, purge it; where it is in error, direct it; where it is superstitious, rectify it; where anything is amiss, reform it; where it is right, strengthen and confirm it; where it is in want, furnish it; where it is divided and rent asunder, make up the breaches thereof, O thou Holy One of Israel: for the sake of Jesus Christ our Lord and Saviour. Amen.

A Blessing of Aedelwald, a Saxon Bishop of the Ninth Century

May God the Father bless us; may Christ take care of us; the Holy Spirit enlighten us all the days of our life.

The Lord be our Defender and Keeper of body and soul, both now and for ever to the ages of ages. Amen.

GRATITUDE FOR GOD'S WORLD

The Opening Prayer

Grant unto us, O God, tonight
> Clear sight to see our own faults;
> Humility to confess and to acknowledge them;
> Resolution to mend and to cure them.

Help us to come to you that you may forgive us for our faults and that you may give us strength and grace to overcome them: through Jesus Christ our Lord.   Amen.

The Reading Lesson: Psalm 65.9-13

7/30/17

Prayer

O God, Creator and Sustainer of all things, we thank you for the world in which we live.

> For night and day;
> For dark and light;
> For summer and winter:
> > We thank you.
> For the sun and the rain and the wind;
> For earth and sea and sky;
> For all the changing seasons of the year:
> > We thank you.
> For all the flowers and fruits and crops of earth;
> For all the wealth which nature offers to man;
> For the beauty and the bounty of this world:
> > We thank you.
> For all that brings nourishment to our bodies and delight to our eyes;
> For all that brings pleasure to our hearts;

> For all the materials which earth gives to our hands on
>   which to work:
>   We thank you, O God.

Grant that everything we see in this world may turn our thoughts to you, the Maker and Creator and Sustainer of it all.

A Prayer of Alcuin

O Eternal Goodness, deliver us from evil. O Eternal Power, be thou our support. Eternal Wisdom, scatter the darkness of our ignorance. Eternal Pity, have mercy upon us. Grant unto us that with all our hearts and minds and strength we may evermore seek thy face; and finally bring us in thine infinite mercy to thy holy presence. So strengthen our weakness that following in the footsteps of thy Blessed Son, we may obtain mercy and enter into thy promised joy: through Jesus Christ our only Saviour and Redeemer. Amen.

The Blessing

The grace of the Lord Jesus Christ be with us all. Amen.

THE TRUE WISDOM

The Opening Prayer

Help us this night, O God, to find the wisdom which will tell us,

> What to do and what not to do;
> When to act and when to refrain from action;
> When to speak and when to keep silent.

So grant that, guided by you, we may be saved from all wrong thoughts, from all words which we would wish unsaid and from all deeds we would wish undone: through Jesus Christ our Lord. Amen.

The Reading Lesson: James 3.6-18 (RSV)

Prayer

Grant unto us this night, O God, to find the wisdom which is from above.

> Give us the wisdom which is pure, that we may never use our minds to think or plan an evil thing;
>
> The wisdom which is peaceable that we may live in friendship with all and in bitterness with none;
>
> The wisdom which is gentle, that we may ever be quicker to sympathize than to criticize, and to praise than to condemn;
>
> The wisdom which is open to reason, that we may not be stubborn and self-willed, but willing to listen to and to obey the truth;
>
> The wisdom which is full of mercy, that we may be as kind to others as we would wish them to be to us;
>
> The wisdom which is full of good fruits, that our lives may be lovely with the beauty of holiness.

A Prayer of Thomas Aquinas

Give us, O Lord, a steadfast heart, which no unworthy affection may drag downwards; give us an unconquered heart, which no tribulation can wear out; give us an upright heart, which no unworthy purpose may tempt aside. Bestow upon us also, O Lord, understanding to know thee, diligence to seek thee, wisdom to find thee, and a faithfulness that may finally embrace thee: through Jesus Christ our Lord. Amen.

The Blessing

The peace of God which passeth all understanding keep our hearts and minds in the knowledge and love of God, and of his Son Jesus Christ our Lord, and the blessing of God Almighty, the Father, the Son and the Holy Spirit, be amongst us and remain with us always. Amen.

FOR PATIENCE

The Opening Prayer

Eternal God, so purify our minds this night that we may think your thoughts after you. So cleanse our hearts that we may love only the things which you command. So touch our lips that we may speak only what you tell us. So strengthen our feet that we may not stumble in the right path. So make lovely our lives that others may see in us the reflection of the Master whose we are and whom we seek to serve: through Jesus Christ our Lord. Amen.

The Reading Lesson: Proverbs 4.1-13

Prayer

O God, give us the patience which we need so much.

Give us patience with people;
Patience with those who need and ask our help;
Patience with those who need our sympathy;
Patience with those who want us to listen while they talk to us.

Give us patience with our work;
Patience to work and study until we make ourselves good craftsmen;
Patience to accept the discipline of learning, of training, and of practice;
Patience to persevere with every task we do until we finish it.

Give us patience with life;
Patience to accept things, even when we do not see either the meaning or the reason for them;

Patience when hopes are very slow to come true;
Patience to take the long view of things and not to be
discouraged.

O God, you are the God of all eternity with all time to work in, help us to learn to wait in patience and in hope.

A Prayer of J. H. Jowett

Our Father, teach us not only to do thy will, but how to do it. Teach us the best way of doing the best thing, lest we spoil the end by unworthy means: for the sake of Christ Jesus our Lord.   Amen.

The Blessing

The grace of the Lord Jesus Christ, the love of God, and the fellowship of the Holy Spirit be with us all now and stay with each one of us always.   Amen.

THE GREATEST OF THESE

The Opening Prayer

Give us now, O God, the reverent mind, that for these few minutes we may forget everything except that you are here. This we ask for your love's sake. Amen.

The Reading Lesson: I Corinthians 13.4-7 in the RSV

Prayer

Let us ask God to give us this love.

Love is patient and kind.

O God, help us to be patient with people even when they are foolish and silly and annoying; and help us always to be as kind to others as we would wish them to be to us.

Love is not jealous or boastful.

O God, help us never to grudge other people their possessions or their successes, but to be as glad as if they were our own; and keep us from all pride and from all conceit that we may never boast of what we are, or have, or have achieved.

Love is not arrogant or rude.

O God, make us at all times courteous, as those who always remember that they are living in the presence of the King; and no matter what we are, and no matter who or what the other person is, help us never to look on anyone with contempt.

Love does not insist on its own way, is not irritable or resentful.

O God, help us,

> Not to sulk when we do not get our own way;
> Not to be irritable and difficult to live with, but to take things and people as they come;

> Not to resent criticism and rebuke, even when we
> think that we do not deserve it.

Love does not rejoice at wrong, but rejoices in the right.

O God, help us never to find any pleasure in any wrong
thing, but to find happiness only in doing the right, and in
helping others to do it.

Love bears all things, believes all things, hopes all things,
endures all things.

O God, help us

> To bear insults, injuries, slights and never to grow bitter;
> Never to lose our faith in Jesus our Lord;
> Never to despair, however dark and difficult and dis-
> couraging life may be;
> To stick it out to the end, and never to give in.

O God, you are love; help us to show your love to others
every day in life. This we ask for your love's sake.   Amen.

The Lord's Prayer in Verse by George Wither, who lived
between 1588 and 1667

> Our Father which in heaven art,
>> We sanctify thy name;
> Thy kingdom come, thy will be done,
>> In heaven and earth the same.
> Give us this day our daily bread,
>> And us forgive thou so,
> As we on them that us offend
>> Forgiveness do bestow.
> Into temptation lead us not,
>> And us from evil free,
> For thine the Kingdom, Power, and Praise
>> Is and shall ever be.

The Blessing

May the blessing of God Almighty, the Father, the Son, and
the Holy Spirit, rest upon us and upon all our work and
worship done in his name. May he give us light to guide us,
courage to support us, and love to unite us, now and evermore.   Amen.

THE LAW OF GOD

The Opening Prayer

O God, help us tonight to be wise enough to ask for your guidance and to be humble enough to take it; to be willing to listen to your commandments, and then to be ready to obey them: through Jesus Christ our Lord. Amen.

The Reading Lesson: Exodus 20.1-17

Prayer

Let us think of God's commandments, and let us ask him to help us to obey each one of them.

You shall have no other gods before me.
O God, help us to give to you and to your obedience the first and the highest place in our lives.

You shall not make yourself a graven image.
O God, help us never to give any man-made thing the first place in our lives, and never to allow the desire for money, fame, power, success to take the place in our hearts and lives which you should have.

You shall not take the name of the Lord your God in vain.
O God, grant that we may never make a statement in your name which is not absolutely true, and grant that we may never make a promise or a pledge in your name and break it.

Remember the Sabbath day to keep it holy.
O God, help us to use your day to help us to live better on the other six days of the week.

Honour your father and your mother.
O God, help us to remember the debt of love and gratitude, of obedience and respect which we owe to our parents, and never to fail to discharge it.

You shall not kill.

Save us, O God, from the anger, the bitterness, the hatred, which would make us wish to hurt or injure any living creature.

You shall not commit adultery.

Keep us, O God, in purity of thought, and word, and action, that we may keep our bodies, and our minds, and our hearts chaste and clean.

You shall not steal.

Keep us, O God, from ever taking that which we have no right to take, and make us so honest that we will never stoop to dishonesty, however slight.

You shall not bear false witness.

Keep us, O God, from all lies and from all untrue words, and especially from repeating the stories and the rumours which would take someone's good name away.

You shall not covet.

Teach us, O God, to be content with what we have, and to serve you with gladness wherever life has placed us.

Help us, O God, to keep these your laws that one day we may receive your reward.

Anselm's Prayer

Grant, O Lord God, that we may cleave to thee without parting, worship thee without wearying, serve thee without failing, faithfully seek thee, happily find thee, for ever possess thee, the one only God, blessed world without end. Amen.

The Blessing

The grace of our Lord Jesus Christ go with us all.   Amen.

THE BLESSEDS OF JESUS

The Opening Prayer

O God, our Father, as tonight we wait on you, grant to us
>> Certainty for our doubts;
>> Strength for our temptations;
>> Power for our tasks;
>> Forgiveness for our sins:
through Jesus Christ our Lord. Amen.

The Reading Lesson: Matthew 5.1-12

Prayer

Let us think of the blessedness of which Jesus taught, and let us ask him to make us able to enter into it.

Blessed are the poor in spirit.
> Help us, O God, to realize our own poverty and our own helplessness, and help us to come to you that you may make us rich in the things which really matter.

Blessed are they that mourn.
> Help us, O God, to be sorry for all the wrong things that we have done, and help us to show that our sorrow is real by not doing them again.

Blessed are the meek.
> Grant to us, O God, such perfect self-control that we may completely master ourselves, so that we may be fit and able to serve and to lead others.

Blessed are they which do hunger and thirst after righteousness.
> Help us, O God, to long for goodness as much as someone starving longs for food, and as much as someone

dying of thirst longs for water, so that we may be ready to do anything and to give up anything to be what we ought to be.

Blessed are the merciful.

O God, our Father, help us at all times to be kind, and help us never either thoughtlessly or deliberately to hurt anyone else; and grant that no one may ever appeal to us for help and not receive it.

Blessed are the pure in heart.

O God, our Father, keep all our thoughts and all our desires clean and pure so that even our secret and inmost hearts may be fit for you to see, and so that we may see you.

Blessed are the peacemakers.

O God, our Father, grant that we may never at any time be the cause of trouble or of quarrels between other people.

Blessed are those who are persecuted for righteousness' sake.

O God, help us to be glad when being a Christian costs us something, because then we have a chance to show that we are not ashamed to let it be seen that we belong to Jesus.

Hear this our prayer and grant us this blessedness, through Jesus Christ our Lord.

A Prayer from Compline

Save us, O Lord, waking, and guard us sleeping, that awake we may watch with Christ, and asleep we may rest in peace: through Jesus Christ our Lord.   Amen.

The Blessing

The grace of our Lord Jesus Christ go with us all.   Amen.

The Opening Prayer

O God, our Father, send out your light and your truth upon us now,

> Your light that we may see where we ought to go;
> Your truth that we may know what we ought to do,

So that, being guided and taught by you we may make no mistakes: through Jesus Christ our Lord. Amen.

The Reading Lesson: Matthew 6.5-14

Prayer

Let us think of Jesus' prayer, and let us make it really ours.

Our Father which art in heaven.

O God, you have taught us to call you Father. Help us to come to you just as easily and just as confidently as we come to our closest friend, sure that you are always ready and willing and able to help.

Hallowed be thy name.

O God, give us the gift of reverence, so that we may remember that, no matter where we are, you see our actions and you hear our words, so that we may with your help make life fit for you to see.

Thy Kingdom come.

O God, help us to do all we can to bring the time when all men will take you as their king, and help us to bring that time nearer by making you king in our own hearts.

Thy will be done in earth as it is in heaven.

O God, whatever happens to us when we try to walk your way, help us to say, Your will be done; and help us to remember that you will never ask us to do anything or to suffer anything except in love.

Forgive us our debts as we forgive our debtors.

O God, help us to forgive others, as we hope ourselves to be forgiven; and help us to remember that we cannot be forgiven, unless we are willing to forgive.

Give us this day our daily bread.

O God, our Father, give us strength and ability to work faithfully and well, so that we may gain the things we need for life. And help us to be grateful for all that we receive and always to share it with others.

Lead us not into temptation, but deliver us from evil.

O God, give us power to resist all our temptations and always to do the right, and, when things are difficult, help us to remember that we will never be tried beyond what we can bear, and that we will never be asked to do what we cannot with your help do.

Erasmus' Prayer

O Lord, Jesus Christ, who art the Way, the Truth, and the Life, we pray thee suffer us not to stray from thee, who art the Way, nor to distrust thee, who art the Truth, nor to rest in any other thing than thee, who art the Life. Teach us by thy Holy Spirit, what to believe, what to do, and wherein to take our rest. Amen.

The Ascription of Thomas Ken and the Blessing

> To God the Father, who first loved us, and made us accepted in the Beloved:
> To God the Son, who loved us, and washed us from our sins in his own blood:
> To God the Holy Spirit, who sheds the love of God abroad within our hearts:
>> Be all love and all glory
>>> For time and for eternity.

And may the blessing of God, Father, Son and Holy Spirit be on us all. Amen.

IN REMEMBRANCE

The Opening Prayer

O God, our Father, we know that we have entered into a
great heritage and a great tradition. We know that we owe
our liberty and our freedom to men who throughout the
years lived and suffered, and sacrificed and died, for truth
and right. Help us this night to remember them with gratitude and to resolve to be worthy of them: through Jesus
Christ our Lord. Amen.

The Reading Lesson: Hebrews 11.32—12.2

Prayer

O God, our Father, we remember all those to whom we
owe the life and the privileges we possess, and we thank you
for them.

For those who lived and suffered and died to give us,
The freedom and good government we possess;
The liberty of conscience and of speech, of thought
and of worship which we enjoy;
We thank you.

For those who lived and suffered and died to find for us,
New continents and new lands and new countries in
the distant places of the earth;
New ways to heal the disease and to ease the pain of
the world;
We thank you.

For all who died in war, on land, at sea, and in the air;
For those who were wounded in body and mind so that
life could never be the same again;

For those who in every age and generation have laid
down their lives for their friends;
> We thank you.

Above all for Jesus, the Captain of every heroic soul;
That he loved us and gave himself for us;
That for us he bore the Cross with all its pain and
shame;
> We thank you.

Help us to remember this night all that this our life has
cost, and help us to resolve never to waste it and never to
soil it.

A Prayer used by Cardinal Newman

O Lord, support us all the day long of this troublous life,
until the shadows lengthen and the evening comes, and the
busy world is hushed, and the fever of life is over and our
work is done. Then, Lord, in thy mercy, grant us a safe
lodging, a holy rest, and peace at the last: through Jesus
Christ our Lord. Amen.

The Blessing

Now may grace, and mercy, and peace from Father, Son
and Holy Spirit, one God, rest upon us all and remain with
each one of us always. Amen.

TO BE SAVED FROM THE FAULTS
THAT SPOIL THE BEST

The Invitation: These words are sometimes found on the doors of old churches.

> Enter this door
> As if the floor
> Within were gold,
> And every wall
> Of jewels all
> Of wealth untold;
> As if a choir
> In robes of fire
> Were singing here.
> Nor shout, nor rush,
> But hush . . .
> For God is here.

Even so let us come to worship God tonight.

The Reading Lesson: II Corinthians 4

Prayer

O God, our Father, keep us from spoiling good things.

> Make us wise,
>> But save us from being conceited.
> Make us clear-sighted,
>> But save us from being unkind.
> Make us honest,
>> But save us from tactless or heartless discourtesy.
> Make us efficient,
>> But save us from being inhuman and unsympathetic.

Make us strong-willed,
    But save us from being stubborn.
Make us to enjoy life,
    But save us from making pleasure our only object
    in life.
Make us pleasant to all,
    But save us from all insincerity.

Help us, O God, to obey the great commandment of Jesus,
and to be perfect, as you, our Father in heaven, are perfect.

A Prayer of Reinhold Niebuhr

O God, give us,
    Serenity to accept what cannot be changed;
    Courage to change what should be changed;
    And wisdom to distinguish the one from the other:
        through Jesus Christ our Lord.   Amen.

The Blessing

The grace of the Lord Jesus Christ be with us all.   Amen.

THE TITLES OF THE CHRISTIAN

The Opening Prayer

O God, our Father, for these few minutes fix our thoughts on you.

> Let no wandering thought distract our attention, and no impure thought keep us from listening.

Help us to worship you tonight with a concentrated attention and a clean heart: through Jesus Christ our Lord. Amen.

The Reading Lesson: II Timothy 2.1-7

Prayer

> Let us think of the titles by which the New
> Testament calls the Christians, that we may
> ask God's help to make them ours.

Jesus' men were called *disciples*, and *disciple* means a *learner*.

> O God, our Father, help us to be wise enough to know that we do not know; and so help us each day to store our minds with some new knowledge. Above all things, help us to know you better every day.

The Christians are called *brothers and sisters*.

> O God, help us as Christians to be brothers and sisters. Grant that we may be able to argue and to differ without quarrelling, and grant that nothing may ever disturb our fellowship.

Jesus called his followers his *friends*.

> O Lord Jesus, help us always to give you the loyalty and the fidelity which true friends ought to give, and help us to prove our friendship by doing what you command us to do.

Christians are to be *lights of the world*.

O God, help us to be a good example to all, that we may ever help them to walk in the right way, and never make it easier for them to go wrong.

Christians are to be *the salt of the earth*.

O God, just as salt gives flavour to things, and keeps things from being tasteless and insipid, help us so to live that we may make life thrilling for ourselves and for others.

Christians are to be good *soldiers*.

Help us, O God, to be always under discipline, always ready to obey the word of your command, always ready to go where you send us, always proud to show whose we are and whom we serve.

Jesus called his followers *apostles*, and *apostle* means *ambassador*.

Lord Jesus, help us at all times to be your ambassadors, so that by our life and our example we may commend to others the faith which our lips profess.

Christians are to be *advertisements* for Jesus.

Lord Jesus, you meant us to be open letters for you, which every one can read; help us always to bring credit and honour, and never discredit and dishonour on the name we bear.

A Prayer of Charles Kingsley

Guide us, teach us, and strengthen us, O Lord, we beseech thee, until we become such as thou wouldst have us to be; pure, gentle, truthful, high-minded, courteous, generous, able, dutiful and useful; for thy honour and glory. Amen.

The Blessing

The blessing of God, the Father, the Son and the Holy Spirit, be on us, and stay with us all. Amen.

TO BE USEFUL AND HELPFUL

The Opening Prayer

O God, our Father, we ask you tonight to
    Strengthen us where we are weak;
    Instruct us where we are ignorant;
    Correct us where we are in error;
    Make us stronger in that which we are already strong.

So grant that we may feel, when this act of worship is done, that it was good for us to have been here: through Jesus Christ our Lord. Amen.

The Reading Lesson: Proverbs 22.1-12

Prayer

O God, our Father, make us the kind of people who are really useful and really helpful.

    Help us, when we are asked, to do with a good grace even that which we do not want to do, and that which no one else will do.

    Help us never to take offence, if someone else is asked to do what we thought we should have been asked to do.

    Help us never to think of praise and prestige, and credit and thanks, so long as the work is done.

    Help us to be equally willing to take the first place and to take the last place.

    Help us, when we are asked to do something, to be more ready to say yes and to say no.

    Help us willingly to use whatever talents you gave us in the service of others.

342

Help us always to be willing to give up time and
pleasure and leisure when someone is required to do
some useful work.

Help us in all things to be like Jesus, amongst our fellow-
men as they who serve. who came not to be served, but to serve.

A Prayer of Archbishop Laud

Lord, here we are, do with us as seemeth best in thine
own eyes, only give us, we humbly beseech thee, a penitent
and a patient spirit to expect thee. Lord, make our service

Lord's PRAYER

acceptable to thee while we live, and our souls ready for
thee when we die: for the sake of Jesus Christ thy Son
our Saviour. Amen.

The Blessing

The grace of our Lord Jesus Christ, and the love of God,
and the fellowship of the Holy Spirit be with us all, and be
with all whom we love here and everywhere, and stay with
each one of us and them this night and always. Amen.

343

THE RIGHT KIND OF LISTENING

The Opening Prayer

O God, our Father, there are so many things within us
which so often keep us from hearing your voice as we
ought:

> The pride, which does not recognize its own need;
> The self-will, which wants no way but its own;
> The wilful blindness, which refuses to see what it does
> not wish to see;
> The wilful deafness, which refuses to hear what it does
> not wish to hear;
> The false independence, which resents advice;
> The foolishness, which thinks that it knows best.

Take from us everything that would keep us from hearing
your voice tonight, and help us to listen, to understand and
to obey: through Jesus Christ our Lord.   Amen.

The Reading Lesson: James 2.14-26

Prayer

O God, a great deal of our life is spent listening to others.
Help us always to listen in the right way.

> Help us to listen with attention,
> > not to let our thoughts wander, to concentrate on what
> > we hear, that it may really stay in our minds, and not
> > go into one ear and out of the other.

> Help us to listen and to understand,
> > Help us not to give up thinking, questioning, enquir-
> > ing, until we really find what a thing means.

Help us to listen and to remember.

Help us not to hear, and then go away and forget all about what we have heard. Give us minds which are interested, for only then can we have memories which are retentive.

Help us to listen and to act.

Help us to put into practice that which we are taught, both at our day's work and at our instruction in the faith. Help us to remember always that words are poor things without deeds, and that faith without works is dead.

And so grant that hearing, understanding, remembering and doing may ever go hand in hand.

A Jewish Prayer

O our Father, grant peace, happiness, and blessing, grace, favour, and mercy, unto all thy people. Bless us, even all of us together, with the light of thy countenance; for by the light of thy face thou hast given us, O Eternal God, the law of life, gracious love, righteousness, blessing, mercy, life, and peace. May it be pleasing in thy sight to bless thy people at all times, and at all seasons with thy peace: for thy Name's sake. Amen.

The Blessing

Unto God's gracious mercy and protection we commit ourselves. The Lord bless us and keep us. The Lord make his face to shine upon us and be gracious unto us. The Lord lift up the light of his countenance upon us, and give us peace, both now and evermore. Amen.

THE VISION OF PEACE

The Opening Prayer

O God, our Father,

Increase our knowledge this night,

that we may know more about you, and more about the life which you want us to live.

Increase our strength of mind and our will-power,

that we may be able better to keep the resolutions that we have made.

Increase our love,

that we may be ever more devoted to Jesus, and that, so loving him more, we may be more true to him, and serve him better.

This we ask for your love's sake. Amen.

The Reading Lesson: Isaiah 11.1-9

We have listened to the vision of the time, when no one shall hurt or destroy, and when all violence and hatred shall cease. Let us pray that we may be able to help to bring that time nearer.

Prayer

O God, our Father, you are the God of peace. Help us to make peace.

Help us to have peace in our relationships with others.

Give us the forbearing and the forgiving spirit. Keep us from being quick to take offence. Control both our temper and our tongue. Help us not to be so quick to condemn what we do not understand, and, when people think differently from us, help us to remember that they too have a right to their opinions, and help us always to treat others as we would have them treat us.

Help us to do all we can to bring peace in the world.

When we meet those of another race or of another colour, or of another party, or of another religion, help us to treat them as friends and not as strangers. Help us to see our nation's greatness, not in mastering other peoples, but in serving them, and in bringing them to a stage when they can take their full and independent place in the life and the work and the councils of the world, not in ruling others, but in helping them to rule themselves.

Help us to do all we can by our prayers, by our conduct, by our words, by our actions, by the giving of money, when money is needed, to bring quickly the day when everyone in the world will know you and love you, so that the day will come when all will know that they are brothers and sisters because you are their one Father.

A Prayer from the Mozarabic Liturgy

O God, who art peace everlasting, whose chosen reward is the gift of peace, and who hast taught us that the peace-makers are thy children, pour thy peace into our souls, that everything discordant may utterly vanish, and all that makes for peace be sweet to us for ever: through Jesus Christ our Lord. Amen.

The Blessing

The peace of God which passeth all understanding keep our hearts and minds in the knowledge and the love of God, and of his Son Jesus Christ our Lord, and the blessing of God Almighty, the Father, the Son, and the Holy Spirit, be amongst us and remain with us always. Amen.

WISDOM TO DECIDE ARIGHT

The Opening Prayer

O God, you can make all things new. Make us new tonight.
  Cleanse our aims and desires,
    that we may never set our hearts on any wrong thing.
  Cleanse our impulses, our emotions and our ambitions,
    that we may never be swept into any wrong action.
  Cleanse our minds and our thoughts,
    that they may never travel down any forbidden path-
    way or linger on any forbidden thing.
  Cleanse our words and our speaking,
    that we may utter no word which we would not wish
    you to hear.
And grant that being cleansed in heart and in mind, we
may pray and think and speak more nearly as we ought:
through Jesus Christ our Lord.   Amen.

The Reading Lesson: Proverbs 17.1-10

Prayer

Give us, O God, the wisdom which will enable us at all
times to know what to do.

  Make us to know,
    When to speak and when to be silent.
      Grant that no cowardice may keep us from speaking
      when we ought to speak, and grant that no angry
      passion may make us speak, when we would regret
      having spoken.

  Make us to know,
    When to say No and when to say Yes.

348

Grant that no weakness may make us yield to, or
agree with, that which is wrong, and grant that no
self-will may make us unreasonably and stubbornly
set on our own way.

Make us to know,
When to criticize and when to praise.
Grant that no too easy tolerance may make us un-
protestingly accept that which is wrong, and that no
ungracious discourtesy may keep us from speaking
the word of encouragement which means so much.

Make us to know,
When to act and when to wait.
Help us to recognize the things which must be done
at once, if they are to be done at all, and to see
what things cannot be hurried and for which we
must in patience wait.

A Prayer of Anselm

We bring before thee, O Lord, the troubles and perils of
people and nations, the sighing of the prisoners and captives, the sorrows of the bereaved, the necessities of
strangers, the helplessness of the weak, the despondency of
the weary, the failing powers of the aged. O Lord, draw
near to each: for the sake of Jesus Christ our Lord. Amen.

The Blessing

The grace of the Lord Jesus Christ be with us all. Amen.

ACKNOWLEDGMENTS

Our grateful thanks are due to the Oxford University Press for the use of two prayers from *Daily Prayer* by E. Milner-White and G. W. Briggs; and one prayer from *A Diary of Private Prayer* by John Baillie; and to Peter Davies Ltd for permission to include a prayer from *Prayers* by Peter Marshall.